Reading & Topic-Discussion Textbook for Intermediate and Advanced Students

# Let's Talk 2

Major New Edition

Written by LIS KOREA Editorial Staff
& Duane Vorhees

LIS KOREA

# Introduction

## *Exploring Darkest English Without Map or Compass*

Over the years, as LIS Korea has continued to produce its ever-expanding line of intelligent conversation guides, many people have asked for answer manuals containing the "right" answers.

With this new edition of **Let't Talk (1) (2)**, the publisher wishes to point out that the purpose of this series is not to restrict the free use of the English language, but to encourage it. English is both richly flexible and difficult for non-native users to learn because of its variability.

Most things can be correctly said in a multitude of ways that reflect the user's personality and situation; at the same time, however, the redundancy of the language generally avoids serious misinterpretation of the user's meaning, even if grievous grammatical mistakes are committed.

People who grow up with the English language are intuitive about its vagaries and, quite frankly, never bother to learn how grammarians want them to use it. Yet they may be extraordinarily expressive and eloquent in their application of it, no matter how far from "proper" they may be.

We want the users of this book to feel confident enough about their genuine ability to communicate in English, no matter how difficult the subject matter or how abstract the thought, that they will simply no longer worry about correct grammar or appropriate usage. Each section is carefully planned to allow great freedom of personal expression while also providing some definitions and explanations to help explain some of the mystery.

For the most part, the grammar is formally correct, but numerous idioms and examples of slang are also provided to indicate the richness and diversity of modern English. Feel free to explore English, boldly and fearlessly. If you get lost somewhere on the journey, don't panic — it's impossible to stay lost for very long. Just keep going ahead, and before you know it you will discover another well-lit, heavily-traficked road, and you'll be safely on your way once again!

**Duane Vorhees**

난산이었다. 계절이 바뀌고 있고, 한해가 저물어가는 것도 느끼지 못하며, 개정판 작업에 매달린 것이 2년여 이제 그 결실을 보게 되었다. 사실 이번 개정판 작업에서 편집진 모두는 여느 때와 달리 더욱 큰 중압감을 느꼈다. 기존 **Let's Talk (1)/(2)**는 (도서출판) 리스 코리아가 출발하면서 처음 내놓은 작품이었다. 이 작품에 대한 독자들의 사랑에 힘입어 리스 코리아가 성장해 나갈 수 있었으며 계속해서 좋은 책을 만들어 나가야 한다는 사명감을 가질 수 있었다. 따라서 더욱 발전된 책으로 보답하고자 하는 편집진의 사명은 이제까지의 어떤 책보다도 훨씬 더 진지했다. 이제 그 결실을 여러 영어학도들에게 내 놓게 됨을 매우 기쁘게 생각하며 여러분들의 격려와 비판의 목소리에 귀 기울이고자 합니다.

## 새롭게 개정된 Let's Talk (1) (2)의 특징은 다음과 같습니다

첫째, 현대인들의 매일매일 생활 속에 들어있는 50 개의 큰 주제 속에 수백개의 작은 질문들을 수록하여 생활 속의 어떠한 주제에 대해서도 대처 할 수 있도록 구성했습니다.

둘째, 특히 What Does It Mean?은 영어학도 여러분들의 기초적인 영어 훈련을 위하여 아주 중요한 섹션이므로 꼭 연습하시기 바랍니다. 영어를 향상시키는데 영어를 영어로 설명하는 훈련보다 더 좋은 방법은 없습니다.

셋째, 이번에 새로운 개정판에서는 기존 책들과 달리 각각의 Opinion Sample에도 질문을 달아 각각의 의견에 대해 또 한번 생각해 보는 기회를 마련 했습니다.

넷째, Part (2)에서는 Part (1) 에서 배운 내용을 다시 실제적인 토론 형식을 빌어 대화체로 구성하여 실제 토론 훈련에 도움이 되도록 했습니다.

다섯째, 책 아래부분에 보여드리는 주석은 책의 좀 어려운 부분을 상세히 쉬운 영어로 설명한 것입니다. 설사 알고 있다고 하더라도 읽어 보시면 많은 도움이 될 것을 확신합니다.

아무쪼록 이책을 통해 독자 여러분의 영어가 한단계 높아지는 계기가 마련되었으면 하는 바람입니다. 또한 이번 기회에 리스 코리아의 책을 사랑해 주시는 독자들에게 말씀 드리고 싶은 것이 있습니다. 많은 독자들께서 Answer Key에 관하여 질문을 많이 하시는데 이책에 포함된 어떠한 질문에도 여러 개의 답이 나올 수 있으며 설사 그 답이 조금 이상하더라도 그것이 큰 문제가 될 것은 없습니다. 이책의 목적은 여러분의 의견을 형성하고 표출하는데 그 목적을 둔 책으로서 책 속의 질문에 근거해서 어떤 말이든지 내 뱉을 수 있다면 이책의 목적은 이미 달성 되었다고 볼 수 있습니다.

이책이 나오기까지 애써주신 모든 분들에게 감사를 드립니다. 집필에 애써주신 리스 코리아 편집진들과 책임 집필자인 Mr. Duane Vorhees 그리고 완벽한 교정을 위해 애써주신 조은예씨에게도 감사의 말씀을 드립니다. 또한 아름다운 그림을 그려주신 박희정씨 그리고 좋은 책이 될 수 있도록 도와주신 예림칼라 디자인 팀 모두에게 감사의 말씀을 드립니다.

리스 코리아 발행인 **최 승 신**

## Major New Edition

***Reading & Topic-Discussion Textbook for Intermediate and Advanced Students***

# *Let's Talk 2*

# CONTENTS

# PART 1

# 25 Everyday Issues

Issue 26



# *Married to a Mama's Boy*

I heard my husband talking on the phone this morning. He said, "Sure, Mom, it's OK... it will be just fine... no problem for us."

After he hung up, I asked him what that was all about, and he hit me with the news that it was his mom's turn to have the annual family party at her house, but she had volunteered our house for the occasion. I got really upset because he didn't even ask me—he just agreed to take it over without consulting me.

I know we will end up paying for all the food and drinks, and nobody in his family will offer to lend a hand in the work involved before, during or after the party. I flew off the handle and told him I would go away for the weekend and he could handle the whole thing himself.

He says I'm overreacting because I hate his family, which is not true. He's got a couple of sisters I'm not crazy about, but I don't hate them. I guess I'm upset because he didn't consult me before agreeing to have the party at our place.

- **hang up :** end a telephone conversation
- **hit :** surprised
- **turn :** time for some action, in rotation
- **volunteer :** say or do (sth) of one's own volition
- **consult :** seek information or advice from (sb)
- **end up :** reach a final state or condition
- **fly off the handle :** become very angry, especially without warning
- **crazy about :** very fond of

## What Does It Mean?

1. mama's boy
2. She had volunteered our house for the occasion.
3. He just agreed to take it over without consulting me.
4. We will end up paying for all the food and drinks.
5. offer to lend a hand
6. I'm overreacting.

## Comprehension

1. What did the man and his mom talk about on the phone?
2. What did he agree to do?
3. Whose turn was it to hold the annual party?
4. Why did the wife get upset when she was told there would be a family party at her house?
5. Does she expect some help from family members in preparing the party?
6. When she became very angry, what did she tell her husband?
7. Does she hate her husband's family?
8. Does she like her husband's sisters?

## Let's Talk!

1. Do you think she should be angry because she wasn't consulted on the matter?
2. Is it right for the wife to go away and let her husband handle the whole thing himself?
3. Do you think he is really a mama's boy?
4. Do you need a "yes" from your spouse before you invite your friends over?
5. What subjects do you consult your spouse about?
6. What subjects do you never consult your spouse about?

## Opinion Samples

**1.** He should have consulted his wife before making the commitment, but I don't think it's good to make a federal case out of it. The fat is in the fire. Anyway, now that the husband said yes to his mom the wife should respect his decision. By cooperating, she will save face for her husband and avert resentment.

*(Q) Should she accept her husband's decision once he has said yes?*

**2.** He is definitely a mama's boy, but his mother is to blame in this case. She should have talked to her daughter-in-law before consulting her son, since throwing a party is generally considered the wife's job. If the wife goes away, it will serve as a serious warning to her husband and his

---

- **commitment :** promise or an obligation
- **make a federal case out of (sth) :** overemphasize the importance of (sth); exaggerate or overreact
- **the fat is in the fire :** (sth) has been done or started that cannot be reversed and will probably have dramatic or serious consequences
- **cooperate :** work together for a common purpose
- **save face :** maintain respect
- **avert :** prevent
- **resentment :** feeling of displeasure or anger because of an insult or other wrong
- **to blame :** at fault
- **throw :** arrange or give (a social event)
- **serve :** act

family and be good preventive medicine against unilateral decisions in the future.

*(Q) Do you think the wife's refusal aggravates her marital relationship?*

**3.** Don't you think the husband has a right to decide on his own to have a family party? I don't understand what's wrong with that. Isn't it natural for him to respect his mother's request? He shouldn't be considered a mama's boy simply because he honors Mom's opinion. The wife's overreacting and making a fuss about nothing.

*(Q) How can you distinguish between a mama's boy and someone who respects his parents' wishes?*

**4.** People talk about women who marry "mama's boys." Let's look at the other side of the coin. What about men who marry "mama's girls"? I have been married for over 25 years, and my wife still has not untied the apron strings. I've felt from the beginning that her mother is more important to her than I am. We have three children and they come ahead of me, too, so I guess you might say I am No. 5.

I could tolerate coming after my kids, but playing second fiddle to my mother-in-law really bothers the dickens out of me. After 25 years, I admit I should be used to it, but I'm tired of being treated like an outsider.

*(Q) Do you think it's natural to give kids priority over one's spouse? Why or why not?*



- **unilateral :** done or undertaken by only one side
- **aggravate :** make (sth) worse
- **overreact :** react to (sth) more strongly than necessary
- **make a fuss about nothing :** complain about (sth) unimportant
- **the other side of the coin :** different or opposite way of thinking about (sth)
- **has not untied the apron string :** has not gotten free of a mother's control
- **tolerate :** put up with (sth); endure
- **play second fiddle :** be in a lower position or rank than (sb)
- **bothers the dickens out of me :** makes me angry; upsets me
- **priority :** higher importance

Issue 27

# Married vs Single

Why do so many people assume↓ that all single people are lonely? This really gets my hackles up.↓ I have been unmarried all my life and I wouldn't have it any other way.

I've seen a number of those so-called wonderful marriages, and all I have to say is, "No, thank you." Married people must account↓ to one another for every living minute. Each has the right to know where the other is at all times, how much money he or she spends and on what.

Marriage demands that everything be shared. Once you are married there is no such thing as "mine." It's all "ours."

I enjoy coming home at night to a quiet, serene↓ house where I can relax. I see and listen to people all day. I don't need to hear any more voices. If I want to talk, there is the telephone. If I want company I have plenty of neighbors and friends. But it's my choice.

I know married women who are lonely as hell, not to mention↓ the ones who are stuck with↓ alcoholics, gamblers, skirt-chasers↓ and sex-maniacs.↓ Surely others must see this, too. I am puzzled as to why so many single women think they are missing so much. Maybe it's because people have a tendency↓ to long for what they don't have instead of counting their blessings.

- **assume :** take (sth) for granted; suppose
- **get (sb's) hackles up :** make (sb) angry
- **account :** explain why (sth) has happened or why (sb) did (sth)
- **serene :** unaffected by disturbance; calm and unruffled
- **not to mention :** phrase used to introduce extra information or emphasize what one is saying
- **stuck with :** unable to get rid of
- **skirt-chaser :** womanizer
- **maniac :** insane person; one who acts in a wildly irresponsible way
- **tendency :** natural disposition to move or act in some direction or toward some result

## What Does It Mean?

1. Married people must account to one another for every living minute.
2. It's my choice.
3. People have a tendency to long for what they don't have instead of counting their blessings.

## Comprehension

1. What kind of prejudice do most folks have about single people?
2. What does the writer name as being married people's obligations?
3. What kind of freedom does the writer think single people enjoy?
4. What is the writer puzzled about?
5. Why do single people think they are missing so much?

## Let's Talk!

1. Why do people marry?
2. Will you marry or remain single?.
3. What do you think about people staying unmarried?
4. Talk about the good things and bad things about marriage.
5. Do you think unmarried people an "odd", "strange" breed?

## Opinion Samples

**1.** I think marriage is hell for both man and woman. But almost always the wife has more responsibility for the children, the home, the dog, and her job, and she is the central emotional prop of the entire family. As if this weren't enough, she has to put up with in-laws, her husband's obnoxious buddies, and his character and personality flaws that he works overtime to conceal from others.

On the other hand, the man also has to pay a high price; he is responsible for the family's bread and butter. He is always under his wife's scrutiny, which limits his freedom. I don't understand why people have to live with these burdens. Being single is the best way to enjoy our lives.

*(Q) Why do many people want to get married in spite of those burdens? Do you think people definitely realize what their responsibilities in marriage will be, before they get married?*

**2.** I'm married because that is probably the best thing for me, especially because of the stability of the relationship. I want and need the warmth and comfort of a relationship—the communicating, growing together, working on problems, enjoying things, nurturing—and receiving. A home around me.

I have been married twenty-eight years and I like it. I like the familiarity, the friendship, having someone special to

- **prop :** (sb) or (sth) that gives help or support to a weak member
- **in-law :** relative by marriage
- **obnoxious :** extremely unpleasant
- **flaw :** defect or imperfection
- **bread and butter :** basic income
- **scrutiny :** close, careful examination or study

love. It's fun and healthful, and it keeps things in perspective. It softens difficult times. It is nice to be wanted and needed. I like marriage. I need and depend upon a wife, good or bad. I love being married. Having a life partner is exciting, fulfilling and comforting. My wife is my backbone in my business. She takes care of everyday problems that I don't want to handle. She is a very good mother to my children, even though she does not turn me on sexually anymore.

Having people around that love you is a very secure feeling. I love my wife and children, and they love me. Home serves as a secure base of operations, a place where I can be me, where I can always come back to, and where I can share my successes and failures. Of course, it's a give-and-take process, and much of the responsibility on my part is listening to my wife also. Marriage is the best arrangement for maintaining security, sanity, child raising, and economic well-being.

*(Q) What do you think this person would say if his wife were an independent professional rather than a traditional homemaker?*

**3.** There is nothing sadder than an unmarried woman. It breaks my heart to see her strolling through the shopping malls, miserably buying exactly what she likes. It's an empty life spending her money and her time as she chooses without worrying what anyone else thinks, needs or wants.

Single women are so wrapped up in themselves, one has to feel sorry for them. They don't have to check with anyone if they decide to see a movie instead of coming home for dinner. They don't fight with anyone over bills, the color of the living room carpet, or at whose house they'll spend the holidays. It's a pretty pathetic picture.

Everyone should be married. No one should be allowed to escape this wonderful experience with its various adjustments.

*(Q) Do you think childless, unmarried people are the happiest in the world or the saddest?*

---

- **keep (sth) in perspective :** judge the importance of (sth) in relation to other issues
- **backbone :** principal support; mainstay
- **give-and-take :** the practice of dealing by mutual compromise
- **wrapped up :** absorbed; involved; bound up
- **pathetic :** causing sympathy or sorrow

**4.** Our society exerts enormous pressure on both men and women to "get married and live happily ever after." Some employers insist on it; they run advertisements which specifically state "Only married men need apply." The implication is that married men are more reliable than single men. But are they? Well, some are and some aren't.

Relatives often view the unmarried member of the family as the odd one. Parents, grandparents, uncles, aunts, and cousins by the dozen are forever looking for "a nice girl." Well-meaning friends never give up trying to put the singleton in double harness. Some singles need and appreciate a friendly assist, but it's a safe bet that when a man reaches the middle thirties without a trace of rice in his hair, he's better off single.

*(Q) Have you ever felt "pressure" to get married from family, friends or society?*

**5.** I don't believe that marriage is good for everyone. Some people should go it alone. I call them non-marriageables and they arrange themselves into distinct categories.

The most obvious non-marriageable personality is the adult who can't cut loose from his parent. This apron-string type is most frequently a male. Every community, no matter how small, has at least one. He is attractive, intelligent, successful, and considered "very eligible." He often dates a lovely woman for several years and tells all within hearing distance that he'd like to marry her some day, but for all kinds of complicated reasons he must wait. Put all his reasons together and they spell MOTHER.

The non-marriageable men who possess excessively aggressive characteristics are the compulsive workers or the

- **exert :** use force or energy
- **well-meaning :** intending or intended to be helpful, but not succeeding
- **singleton :** unmarried person
- **in double harness :** "hitched" (married)
- **a safe bet :** (sth) that is likely to happen
- **rice in (one's) hair :** being married; refers to custom of throwing rice at a newly married couple
- **better off :** in an improved condition
- **cut loose :** become free; independent
- **apron-string type :** controlled, influenced, or dominated too much by one's mother
- **eligible :** qualified or suited
- **compulsive :** having a strong, irresistible impulse

money grubbers. The compulsive worker can be a scientist, a newspaper editor, a politician, or an artist, but usually he's a businessman. He eats, sleeps, and dreams his career. It is not money that motivates him; in fact he frequently passes up more lucrative opportunities to stay with the work he loves. He would rather work than eat or sleep, and often this is precisely what he does. Such a man is better off single. He contributes little to marriage, and it is difficult for any wife to settle for the crumbs.

On the other hand, the money grubber can often fool a woman. She is deluded into thinking he'll make a good husband because he is obviously headed for financial success. He's dynamic, aggressive, indefatigable and imaginative, all fine qualities. But they can be destructive when not balanced by a decent set of values.

The most easily recognized non-marriageable female is the wildly competitive type. The competitive woman is usually successful in business or a profession. She is competent, driven and domineering. Her theme song is "Anything You Can Do, I Can Do Better." She hails the taxi, orders the dinner, finishes the man's sentences for him and wants to lead on the dance floor. She pours a great deal of her energy into her work and finds her major satisfaction in the feeling of importance that it gives her. She makes a lively dinner companion but a horrible wife. To her a man is an audience, a whipping boy, an object of her hostility, and sometimes a willing slave.

*(Q) How can we distinguish between the marriageables and non-marriageables?*



- **money-grabber :** (sb) who is aggressively engaged in or preoccupied with making or saving money
- **pass up :** let (sth) good go by
- **crumb :** remnants
- **fool :** deceive or trick (sb); mislead
- **deluded :** deceived
- **indefatigable :** incapable of being tired
- **hail :** signal, call, summon
- **finish (sb's) sentences :** interrupt, do (sb's) talking for (sb)
- **whipping boy :** target of abuse; (sb) who is made to bear the blame for another's mistake; scapegoat

Issue 28

# For Men & Women

–Tell your sweetheart you love her. She can never hear it too often.

–If you like the way she looks, dresses, talks, smells, let her know it. But if you don't like something about her, keep it to yourself!

–Never try to make her jealous.

–Treat her with the same respect and courtesy you show women you don't know well.

–In addition to remembering her on all the usual gift-giving occasions, such as birthdays, anniversaries, or Christmas, from time to time surprise her with a little gift for no reason at all.

–If you've had an especially wonderful evening together, send her flowers or a single rose the next morning. If she's a working woman, send it to her place of employment. She will appreciate it twice as much.

–When you are at a party together, never leave her alone while you're off talking with someone else.

–Tell her she is absolutely the most wonderful person in the world, and she'll believe that you are.

–If you want to be loved, be loving. Be nice to her relatives and they'll tell her how lucky she is to have you.

* * * * *

–Tell him often that you love him. If you're married, don't ask him if he loves you, or he's liable to say, "I married you, didn't I?"

–Never criticize him in public. If you do have a criticism, be sure it's constructive and offered in the spirit of love and helpfulness, not in anger or as a put-down.

–Don't bad-mouth his friends or worse yet, his relatives.

–Never keep him waiting. If he has a tendency to be late, always have something in your purse to read. It makes the waiting more tolerable, and you will be less apt to chew him out when he finally shows up.

–Don't call him at work unless it's absolutely necessary.

- **courtesy :** polite behavior; an act or gesture showing politeness
- **liable :** likely
- **constructive :** serving a useful purpose or helping to improve (sth)
- **put-down :** criticism or insult
- **bad-mouth :** criticize (sb), often unfairly or spitefully

–Every man needs a desk, a closet or a cupboard to call his own. Don't try to tidy it up for him even though it's a cluttered mess and an eyesore.
–If he eats—or drinks—a little too much, don't nag him about it. But do remind him in a loving way you wish he'd take better care of himself because you'd like to have him around to grow old and gray with.
–Never quiz him about where he's been or with whom.
–Don't sulk. If something's bugging you, talk it out and clear the air. If he asks what's eating you, don't say "Nothing" or "You should know."
–Never lie to him. If there is something you prefer not to tell him, keep quiet. But if you tell him something, be sure it's the truth.
–Keep yourself clean from head to toe.
–Develop some interests other than just him. The more outside interests you have, the more interesting to him you'll be.
–Surprise him occasionally. A little love note left on his pillow, in his lunch pail or briefcase will warm his heart.



## What Does It Mean?

QUES...

1. If you do have a criticism, be sure it's constructive.
2. chew him out
3. Talk it out and clear the air.

## Comprehension

QUES...

1. Why do you think receiving flowers at her workplace would make her happy?
2. If she wants to criticize him, what should she do?
3. If he overdrinks, what shouldn't she do?

- **tidy up :** put in order; make neat
- **clutter :** fill with things in a disorderly manner
- **sulk :** show that (sb) is angry about being treated badly by looking unhappy and not talking to anyone
- **bug :** annoy, trouble, or pester (sb)
- **eating :** bothering

## Let's Talk!

1. How often do you tell your sweetheart "I love you"? Do you think it's easy to say it often? If not, how can you make it a habit?
2. Men are usually expected to remember birthdays and anniversaries on their own and give presents to women on these occasions, but women are not under the same obligation. Why? Do you think it's fair?
3. If your sweetheart is almost always late for an appointment, how should you cope with the situation? How about if you are the one who's usually late—what should you do?
4. Should there be any difference between men and women in terms of smoking and drinking?
5. How are men and women different? List as many differences as you can.



## Opinion Samples

**1.** There was a time, once, when women had no social functions other than wife and mother. They stayed mainly at home and had no money of their own. Their husband or father was a domestic despot who made all the decisions. But they were nonetheless human beings, and the men who loved them felt the obligation to recognize their special service from time to time by celebrating their birthday or anniversary. For two or three days a year, they were rewarded for all the other days when they were little more than slaves. Those days have passed! Nearly as many women work as men, and they have their own roles to play outside the home. And they have their own incomes. It is often the case that the husband uses most of his salary to maintain the household, while the wife keeps most of hers. While it is true that the women are still expected to take care of the house and children, at least they get to spend a good deal of time at home (and, indeed, their husbands probably pays for a housekeeper to do the work in their stead), but men's work still tends to keep them away from home for most of

→ **despot :** (sb) who wields power oppressively; a tyrant
→ **in (sb's) stead :** in place of (sb)

the day.

The time has come for women to recognize how hard their men work on their behalf. Instead of expecting expensive gifts (jewelry and the like) for their birthdays, they should start recognizing their husbands' worth. Even if it is only once or twice per annum, they should treat their self-sacrificing hubbies with more than just respect and affection. Take him out, give him something that he can show off to his pals and workmates, make him realize that he is loved and appreciated.

*(Q) Who do you think leads a more stressful life, the modern man or the contemporary woman?*

**2.** Smoking and drinking are social vices. They do more harm than good. In moderation, probably neither activity is especially harmful. But most people who engage in them do not do so moderately. Having said this, there should not be different standards between the ways men and women behave. Culturally, biologically, they are essentially the same: they are human beings. If it is OK for men to smoke or drink, it should be equally all right for women to do so. (A special case might be made that pregnant women should refrain, since the babies in their wombs may be adversely affected; but, otherwise, there should be no difference.) The time has long passed when women were considered to be somehow "morally superior" to men, or "the weaker sex" that needs to be protected. The double standard that has prevailed for so long needs to be abolished: men should not have the "right" to have extramarital affairs or abuse their health, unless women have the same rights.

*(Q) Do you think women are the weaker sex? Why or why not?*

- **per annum :** by the year; yearly
- **vice :** evil or immoral behavior
- **in moderation :** within reasonable or sensible limits
- **refrain :** stop oneself from doing (sth)
- **adverse :** not favorable; going against or in an opposite direction
- **double standard :** set of principles applied differently to one group of people than to another
- **prevail :** be most common; be in use; be current
- **abolish :** end (sth) completely
- **extramarital :** relating to sexual relations with someone other than (one's) spouse

Issue 29

# *Money and Friends*

Some time ago, I loaned $1,000 to a couple I considered to be my closest friends. Their money was tied up in a court dispute with a business partner, and they needed financial assistance for living expenses.

I didn't have much excess cash sitting around, but I offered them my income tax refund because I knew they were desperate. They promised to pay me back within 90 days.

The due date came and went. They didn't send the money, and I didn't hear a word from them. When I asked them to repay the loan soon, they assured me that the money would be in my hands within two weeks. After two weeks no money was sent and no explanation was given. When I phoned to say I really needed that $1,000, I was informed rather brusquely that they would give me the money when they could.

It's been six months since I first told them I needed that money. I have written twice to let them know that I understand things are tight and that they are probably embarrassed. I asked if we could work out some sort of repayment schedule. So far they haven't replied. I've left messages on their answering machine, but there has been no response.

Short of legal action, I don't know what else to do to get my money back and still retain our friendship. Needless to say, I'm deeply disappointed that my good friends would treat me this way.

- **tax refund :** money returned from overpayment of taxes
- **brusque :** rudely abrupt in manner or speech; blunt
- **short of (sth) :** without actually doing (sth)

## What Does It Mean?

1. Their money was tied up in a court dispute.
2. excess cash sitting around
3. They were desperate.
4. due date
5. Things are tight.
6. We could work out some sort of repayment schedule.
7. short of legal action



## Comprehension

1. How much did he lend to his friends?
2. How did he get the money for them even though he had no excess cash on hand?
3. After they broke the payment schedule twice, what did they finally say?

## Let's Talk!

1. Do you believe that if you lend money to your friend, then you will lose both your friend and your money?
2. Do you think it's OK to charge your friend reasonable interest on any money you lend?
3. If your friend refused to pay you back, would you take him to court?↓
4. Would you lend money to a friend? Why or why not?
5. Would you ask your friend for money if you were in financial trouble?

## Opinion Samples

**1.** I never "lend" money to my friends. This means that if my friend asked for money I would give him the exact amount of money I could afford without expecting him to pay me back, and never more than I could afford to lose. Then I could maintain the friendship and not feel resentful if I didn't get the money back. If my friend asked for more money than I could safely handle, I would simply refuse to give it.

*(Q) What if your friend became estranged from you because you wouldn't loan him money? How would you feel?*

→ **take (sb) to court :** begin legal proceedings against (sb); sue

**2.** We see many cases of good friendship eroded by money. However, if we think someone is a true friend and he or she is in trouble financially, why not lend money? Friendship cannot be bought by money, but it can be thrown away by a lack of generosity.

*(Q) Would you be disappointed if your friend refused to lend money to you?*

**3.** The following rhyme describes a loan dilemma between friends.

I had some money
And a friend.
I loaned my money
To my friend.
I lost my money
And my friend.

This is not to say one must never lend money to a friend; but sad to say, more often than not it sours the relationship.

*(Q) Who is more to blame when friendship sours, due to a dispute over money, the lender or the borrower?*



- **eroded :** reduced
- **more often than not :** in most situations
- **sour :** become unpleasant or less friendly

Issue 30

# Getting Rich Quick

My husband and I put our life savings into a sure-fire business venture. A smooth-talking gentleman we knew told us we would make a fortune. This fellow sold manufacturing equipment, and he talked us into starting a small plant. We were to buy the machines from him, and he would teach us how to run the business. He even offered to hire an experienced factory manager.

I could write a book on what happened. The machines quickly broke down, and we had to buy new parts, which cost us a lot of money we hadn't planned on spending. The plant manager that he hired turned out to be an alcoholic who stayed home three days a week. My husband and I both put in 12-, 14-hour days, and we worked like slaves. At the end of seven months we were broke and the business was in debt. We had to mortgage our home and borrow money from my father-in-law. Three months later we were broke again. So, the man who talked us into the business offered to buy us out for 10 cents on the dollar. And we had no choice but to accept. Today, that man is running the plant himself and making money hand over fist. We later learned he owns four other factories which he took over in the same way. We've consulted a lawyer, but legally the man is on safe ground.

In the aftermath, my husband has developed high blood pressure and ulcers. Being around our kids makes him nervous, and he hasn't spoken a civil word to me in weeks. We're still deeply in debt, and a lot of our old friends avoid us. The whole episode just makes me sick!



- **sure-fire :** certain to be successful
- **turn out :** end up; result
- **broke :** without money
- **mortgage :** loan using real estate as collateral
- **hand over fist :** quickly and abundantly
- **aftermath :** consequence or result, especially of a disaster or misfortune

## What Does It Mean?

1. I could write a book on what happened.
2. Legally the man is on safe ground.

## Comprehension

1. What kind of business did the couple go into?
2. What happened to their business? What happened to them?
3. What happened to the man when he took over their factory?



## Let's Talk!

1. Who do you think is more responsible for the consequences, the man or the couple?
2. What did the couple do wrong, if anything? Was it just bad luck?
3. Do you think the man has a guilty conscience? Should he? Why or why not?
4. How can the couple get even with the man? What would you do?
5. How could you avoid having the couple's problems, do you think?
6. Is there any quick, sure way to make a fortune? If so, what is it? If not, why not?

get even : get revenge; retaliate; strike back

## Opinion Samples

**1.** Laws should be passed to protect the public from false claims. Of course, people should be given the means to gain access to the truth, so they can make decisions based on accurate information. But, in the end, people must accept the consequences of their own folly. No one should ever invest his entire life savings in any scheme in which he does not have sound, first-hand experience. No one should ever be surprised if his business fails, even if he has done everything right. There are no "sure things," no "short cuts" to genuine success. All is risk; the best we can do is lower the risk as far as possible, by applying common sense and expertise to the problem at hand, and then taking our chances.

*(Q) Who succeeds and who fails in business?*

**2.** What the smooth-talker did to her husband was reprehensible, but what her husband is doing to himself is worse. Fortunes are made and lost every day. When businessmen go bankrupt, some commit suicide, others make themselves sick with worry. But still others pick themselves up, dust themselves off and go on. The ability to roll with the punches is what separates the men from the boys, and the women from the girls.

*(Q) Who is able to get over life's challenges — and who cannot?*

**3.** Most of us have been victimized in one way or another by some unscrupulous opportunist. Even experienced people can be taken in by clever operators. In

- **false claim :** untruthful assertion
- **folly :** foolish act or idea
- **scheme :** plan of action; project or system
- **sound :** sensible; valid
- **first-hand :** direct from the source
- **short cut :** the quickest or most direct path; policy or practice that reduces the time or energy needed to accomplish (sth)
- **expertise :** expert advice, opinion, skill, or knowledge
- **take chances :** do (sth) even though it involves risk
- **reprehensible :** worthy of blame
- **bankrupt :** unable to pay one's debts due to lack of money
- **roll with punches :** recover from being hit without being knocked down or injured
- **victimize :** cause (sb) to become harmed by (sb else)
- **unscrupulous :** dishonorable
- **opportunist :** (sb) who uses every chance to gain power or advantages, even if dishonestly
- **take in :** trick or deceive (sb)

many instances, we can't control what happens to us, but we can control our own reactions to what happens to us.

*(Q) How do you try to cope in the face of failure?*

**4.** It would be a wonderful world if all men were honest and decent, but they aren't, and there's no evidence that they ever will be. So we need to be aware that we will always be surrounded by liars, crooks, gossips, and bigots, who often prosper in spite of their immorality. Unfortunately, it too often appears that good fortune smiles with special favor on the unconscionable scoundrel who climbs to success on the broken backs of others.

*(Q) Do you agree? If so, what do you think is the role of God in maintaining justice?*

**5.** Knowledge is power, but whim holds power over most of us. That is why advertisers and con men base their appeals on impulse rather than intellect. Information is the surest way to avoid being ripped off, by circumstance or design. In this particular case, the couple had apparently been saving money for their future for some time—a wise move, especially in light of their subsequent actions. For they lacked an understanding of the basic nature of the business they owned, they did not have any business sense or management skills, they maneuvered themselves into a tighter and tighter financial corner, and they never learned how to cut their losses—until there was no more to lose. A strong dose of skepticism would have been their best medicine from beginning to end of their unfortunate venture.

*(Q) Is there any difference between men and women in terms of buying attitude?*



- **crook :** (sb) who gets money dishonestly; criminal
- **bigot :** (sb) who is intolerant of those with different identities, esp. religious, racial, or national
- **unconscionable :** without conscience; without morality
- **scoundrel :** wicked or dishonorable person; villain
- **whim :** sudden idea, thought, or wish to do (sth) without forethought
- **con men :** confidence men; scam artists; people who make money by promoting fraudulent schemes
- **impulse :** sudden desire leading to action
- **rip off :** cheat or take (sth) from (sb) dishonestly
- **by design :** purposefully
- **subsequent :** following (sth) else in time or order
- **maneuver :** manage or direct (sb) or (sth), especially by guile

Issue 31

# Lessons for Life

– You are responsible for your own happiness.
– No one can diminish your self-esteem unless you give them permission to do so.
– People won't stay mad at you for long if you can say I blew it, and I'll try to make amends.
– When something is troubling you, talk about it to people you trust instead of trying to cover it up. You may be surprised to find that they have been through something similar.
– Don't pass up an opportunity to tell people you care about them. You may never get another chance.
– Reserve judgment until you know all the facts. Even then, keep your mouth shut if no useful purpose will be served by adding your two cents' worth.
– Be grateful for your good health and the health of those you love.
– Be aware that without good health, wealth and success mean little.
– If you enjoy your work and your life, you are rich. If you aren't happy with either, how can money help?
– If you have had a rotten day, don't take it out on others. Simply say tomorrow is sure to be better.
– Don't be afraid to try what you think you can't do. However, if you fail, leave from your mistakes and try again.
– Try to put together the best overall package of ambition, kindness, consideration, self-esteem and intelligence you can. Otherwise, you'll spend your life alone.
– Spend time with your spouse and children.
– You can respect and learn from people even if you don't like them. You can learn something from anyone, because every person in the world knows something that you don't.

- **diminish :** make or become smaller; reduce or decrease
- **blow :** mishandle, ruin or bungle
- **make amends :** pay back or compensate, as for an injury, loss, or insult
- **been through :** experienced
- **pass up :** let (sth) good go by
- **reserve :** save (sth) for a particular purpose or later use
- **take it out on :** treat (sb) badly because of anger at (sth) else

## What Does It Mean?

1. I blew it.
2. two cents' worth
3. take it out on others

## Comprehension

1. What attitude should we cultivate to deal with having a rotten day?
2. Why can we always learn something from others?



## Let's Talk!

1. In terms of advice, do you usually give it or seek it?
2. What have you learned from your parents?
3. What have you learned from your friends?
4. What have you learned from your spouse?
5. What have you learned from your teachers?
6. What have you learned from your boss?
7. What are the most important lessons in life you've learned so far?
8. "We ask advice, but we want approbation." Do you agree with that saying? Why or why not?
9. We say, "Nobody can give you better advice than yourself." Explain what it means. Why is that so?
10. What are life's lessons that you want to teach your children?

---

approbation : approval; praise

## More Talking Points

**What advice would you give the following people?**

(a) Heavy smoker
(b) Heavy drinker
(c) Cheapskate
(d) Henpecked husband
(e) Divorcing couple
(f) Mama's boy
(g) Gold digger
(h) Cheater
(i) One who thinks love is everything in marriage
(j) One who thinks money isn't important in life
(k) Lottery winner
(l) One who is about to drop out of college
(m) Someone who thinks his life was ruined by his friends
(n) One who wants to commit suicide

→ **gold digger :** woman who intends to use her sexual charm for material gain, esp. by marrying (sb) who is better off financially

## Opinion Samples

**1.** When we ask our friends for advice, we really want them to agree with our actions. If they tell us we were wrong to behave as we have done, we react with astonishment and scorn. If they respond sympathetically, we not only feel justified but happy in the wisdom of our friends. This hunger for approbation is probably strongest when we feel the most doubt about our own actions; if we are genuinely comfortable with our decision, we don't need external approval. A good conscience sleeps soundly, but a doubtful one will disturb the entire night.

*(Q) What was the best and worst advice you've ever given?*

**2.** An ongoing debate within liberal democratic governments is where to draw the line between freedom and authority. Well-meaning officials may seek to pursue policies that are in the public interest, based on expert analysis. Oftentimes, these programs will prove highly successful in accomplishing their purposes, and areas such as environmental protection, civil rights, and education have benefited greatly from social intervention. On the other hand, intelligent people know their own interests better than any outsider possibly can and resent interference that limits their ability to solve their own problems in their own way.

*(Q) Are there any personal behaviors, that do not harm anyone else, which society has the right to regulate?*



→ **sympathetic :** in harmony or agreeing with (one's) taste, mood, or nature
→ **draw the line :** mark the limit

Issue 32

# How to Raise Your Child

Remember that a child is a gift from God, the richest of all blessings. Do not try to mold him in the image of yourself, your father, your mother, your brother or your neighbor. Each child is an individual and should be permitted to be himself.

Don't crush a child's spirit when he fails. And never compare him with others who have done better. Remember that anger and hostility are natural emotions. Help your child find socially acceptable outlets for these feelings, or they may be turned inward and create physical or emotional problems.

Discipline your child with firmness and reason. Don't let your anger throw you off balance. If he knows you are fair, he will not lose his respect or his love for you. Make sure the punishment fits "the crime." Even the youngest of children has a keen sense of justice. And make sure you and your spouse maintain a united front. Never join with your child against your husband or your wife. This creates emotional conflict and generates destructive feelings of guilt, confusion and insecurity.

Do not give your child everything his little heart desires. Instead, show him how to attain it on his own. Allow him to know the thrill that comes from earning something. Do not deny him the greatest pleasure of all, the satisfaction that comes with self-achievement, the knowledge he deserves what he has.

Do not set yourself up as a model of perfection. You will find it easier to communicate with your child if he knows that Mom and Pop can make mistakes, too.

Don't make threats in anger or glowing promises when you are in a generous mood. Threaten or promise only what you can deliver, and then make sure that you do so. To a child, a parent's word means everything. If he loses his faith in his parents, he will have difficulty believing in anything.

- **crush :** overwhelm; destroy completely
- **outlet :** means of releasing energies
- **keen :** eager; interested; enthusiastic
- **glowing :** highly favorable

On the other hand, do not smother your child with gifts and lavish surprises. The purest and the healthiest love expresses itself in discipline day-in, day-out. Consistency builds self-confidence, trust and a strong base for character development.

Teach your child that there is dignity in hard work, whether it is performed with a shovel or with delicate fingers that hold surgical instruments or push computer keys. Let him know that a useful life is a rewarding one and that a life of ease and pleasure-seeking is empty and meaningless.

Do not try to protect your child against every blow and disappointment. Allow him to get his lumps when they come. Adversity strengthens character and creates compassion. Trouble is the great equalizer, the common denominator of living. He is bound to have some trouble in his life. He must learn how to handle it.



## What Does It Mean?

1. Help your child find socially acceptable outlets for these feelings.
2. They may be turned inward.
3. Make sure the punishment fits "the crime."
4. Never join with your child against your husband or your wife.
5. glowing promises when in a generous mood

## Comprehension

1. What will happen if we repress a child's anger and hostility?
2. What role does adversity play in character development?

- **smother :** lavish attention on (sb); enfold
- **blow :** sudden unexpected shock or piece of bad luck
- **lumps :** bad things that happen
- **equalizer :** (sth) that affects all people or groups the same way
- **denominator :** that which determines
- **repress :** hold (sth) back

## Let's Talk!

1. What attitude is the most important for your child to learn from you?
2. What attitude do you most want your child not to learn from you?
3. How hard is it for you to avoid comparing your child with others?
4. When should you praise your child?
5. When should you criticize him?
6. When should you give him a present?
7. What is your rule about giving pocket money to children?
8. Do you think your child loves and respects you? Why or why not?
9. What is your recipe for raising a child?
10. What worries you most about your child?
11. What life philosophy do you want your child to have?

## Opinion Samples

**1.** There are only two kinds of standards, normative and objective, and we all use both of them all the time. An example of an objective standard would be to declare that anyone who gets 90% of the answers correct on a math test has an A. Perhaps no one will get an A, maybe everyone will. Normative standards are comparative: anyone in the top 10% of the class, in terms of the number of correct answers, gets an A. On some tests, students scoring a 95% may not qualify for an A, and on others perhaps none of the A's are higher than 85%.

The same is true for our children. Sometimes we evaluate them on the basis of objective standards (being able to count to 100, being able to recite the entire alphabet), and other times we do so on the basis of how quickly, or how early, that task is accomplished.

*(Q) Which is more fair, do you think, a normative or an objective test?*

**2.** To be a success, everyone should strive to be either the smartest person or the best-liked one. The former is the most difficult task, and few should even attempt it; but the winners will do very well indeed. The latter, however, is within the grasp of everyone, and the winners will lead happy, fulfilled lives.

*(Q) How can you become better-liked than you are?*



- **normative :** describing or establishing a set of rules or standards of behavior in relative terms
- **qualify :** show that one has the ability for (sth)
- **grasp :** the ability to get (sth); reach

Issue 33

# Stop Berating Yourself

To you and the thousands of other parents who are miserable because of what you have done to your children, I say this: Stop berating yourselves. You did the best you could with the tools at hand: inexperience, clay feet, the works. No one knows why some children turn out to be champions in spite of parents who provide precious little emotional nourishment, while other kids, who are loved, wanted, tenderly nurtured, and have all the so-called advantages, turn out perverse, estranged and unable to cope with life.

I have come to believe in the genetic factor, though this has been ignored by many modern behavioral scientists. We all inherit our nervous systems, and if the nervous system is fragile, it places severe limitations on what a person can tolerate. Certain individuals are born survivors. They can withstand life's harshest blows and emerge the stronger as a result. Others crumble in the face of minor adversity. The same fire that melts butter can make steel strong.

And let us not overlook personal responsibility. I am sick of hearing children blame their parents for messing up their lives. People with all sorts of handicaps can and do make it in this demanding and competitive world.

For those who are hooked on dope, there are drug-abuse centers with trained personnel, eager and waiting

- **berate :** scold severely
- **clay feet :** weak foundation
- **the works :** everything
- **perverse :** stubbornly opposing or resisting what is right, expected, or reasonable
- **estranged :** not feeling any connection with (sth) that used to be important in (one's) life
- **genetic :** relating to genes
- **gene :** the basic physical unit of heredity
- **fragile :** easily damaged or broken; frail
- **crumble :** collapse into crumbs; lose power, become weak, or fail
- **overlook :** fail to notice or consider
- **mess up :** spoil or ruin
- **dope :** narcotic or other drug, especially one sold and used illegally

to help. For individuals who need professional counseling, there are mental-health clinics. The self-help groups do a remarkable job getting people to take control of their lives; and they are free!

Enough of this "You damaged me, now take care of me" nonsense. It's a cop-out! The parental guilt our kids try to lay on us is so thick you can cut it with a knife. But it serves no purpose except to perpetuate financial and emotional dependence and create a climate of hostility, punishment and ultimate failure. God helps those who help themselves.

## What Does It Mean?

1. Stop berating yourselves.
2. The same fire that melts butter can make steel strong.
3. Parental guilt laid on by our kids is so thick you can cut it with a knife.

## Comprehension

1. What determines if our children become successful or not?
2. How many psychologists believe that genetic factors are the key to character?
3. What's wrong with someone who blames his parents for his screwed-up life?



- **self-help groups :** group of people with a particular problem who help each other
- **cop-out :** act of avoiding responsibility
- **ultimate :** final; last
- **screwed-up :** ruined

## Let's Talk!

1. What is the most important factor in a successful life?
2. How do some children from poor or single-parent families manage to become successful?
3. Some children from rich families who get good educations fail dreadfully. Why?
4. How can we instill a sense of personal responsibility in our children?
5. What's your definition of a "successful life"?
6. How did your parents bring you up? Give examples.
7. Do your children agree with your philosophy of life? Is that good or bad?

## Opinion Samples

**1.** There's nothing like a little deprivation in life—and the determination to do better—to spur one to greater effort. If you have to scrap for every scrap* of food, you soon learn to fight or starve. These lessons are hard, but effective. Native talent and intelligence are indeed fine tools to have, but they pale beside motivation in achieving success—and there is no motivation like lack of choice. If your back is against the wall, you can't run, you can't hide. You have to fight or die. This is not a very noble philosophy, but in the end it is all that matters.

*(Q) Is life only a struggle for survival, or do other things matter too?*

**2.** Nothing in life is guaranteed. We may have fine parents and good health. We can have money and high IQs. It might seem like we have everything. But unless we are lucky, none of it matters. There is nothing like being the right person in the right place at the right time. Of course, how one uses the opportunity available is important, too, and we can all prepare ourselves for that moment, if and when it comes. But if The Right Moment doesn't come, there's not much we can do.

*(Q) Who determines our destiny? God or ourselves?*



- **deprivation :** lack of (sth) that (sb) needs or wants
- **scrap :** fight, esp. with fists
- **scrap* :** small piece; fragment
- **pale :** become less important relative to (sth)
- **matter :** be of importance

Issue 34

# Part-time Job

My husband and I have been arguing about something for several weeks. We need the opinion of an unbiased outsider.

Our son is 17. He wants to work in a shopping mall after school and on weekends. Several of his friends are employed there. They make only a few dollars an hour. We are upper-middle-class people. Our son gets an allowance and does not need to work. I'm opposed to his taking this job because his grades are only fair and if he works they will get worse.

His father says our son needs the discipline that a job will provide, plus it will teach him how to handle money. He keeps reminding me that he worked at various jobs after school starting when he was 14, and they prepared him for a successful career. Which one of us is right?

- **unbiased :** without prejudice; impartial
- **discipline :** training expected to produce a specific skill, behavior, or character

## What Does It Mean?

1. We need the opinion of an unbiased outsider.
2. needs the discipline that a job will provide

## Comprehension

1. What have the couple been arguing about?
2. What do they need now?
3. What does their son want to do?
4. How much can their son make if he works in the mall?
5. Why is the mother opposed to her son's working?
6. What are the reasons her husband says their son should work?

## Let's Talk!

1. Who is right, the husband or the wife?
2. Talk about the good and bad things about youngsters having part-time jobs.
3. What kind of part-time jobs do you think are right for teenagers? For college students?
4. Do you think teenagers can successfully balance work and study?
5. Do you think they have a right to spend the money they make any way they wish?
6. How can we teach our children the value of money?
7. How do you (or your children) get pocket money?

## Opinion Samples

**1.** There is a great deal of validity in what her husband says, but a teenager's principal job should be studying. If he is doing no better than "fair," it would be foolish to let him work in the mall. Too often school work suffers when mediocre students take on part-time employment, and frequently their paychecks go for motorbikes, secondhand cars, record albums, leather jackets, drugs, and alcohol.

In many homes it is essential for teenagers to work to help buy food and clothing for the family or save up for college. But in affluent cases like this, the wife should tell her husband to forget it.

*(Q) Should adults let young children work to support the family financially?*

**2.** I think there is nothing to worry about if the boy has a part-time job. He is 17, so he is old enough to balance his studies and his work. I agree with her husband: he needs to learn how difficult and how precious it is to make money. This will give him good sense and practice in spending money. I think that practical knowledge is more important for him at his age than the more academic knowledge he gets in school.

*(Q) How does practical knowledge complement academic knowledge?*



- **validity :** truth
- **mediocre :** neither good nor bad; average; ordinary
- **affluent :** rich enough

Issue 35

# Before Getting Married

Some people unjustly regard with contempt unmarried couples who are living together.

After dating for three years, my boyfriend and I moved in together to minimize living expenses. We planned to get married after I graduated from college.

Well, my family practically disowned me when we told them we were living together! (His folks were more broad-minded about it.)

After we had lived together for a year I found out he had a terrible temper. On the day he grabbed me by my blouse and threw me against the wall so hard I thought my shoulder was broken, I walked out on him. I thank God I didn't marry him. What a fix I'd have been in if, after we were married and had a child, I had learned that he was capable of physically abusing any of us!

So, the next man I fall in love with I will make sure I live with before making a lifetime commitment. Living together before marriage may be a "sin," but it's the only way one can really get to know a person before it's too late.

- **unjust :** violating principles of justice or fairness; unfair
- **disown :** refuse to acknowledge responsibility for
- **walk out on :** desert; leave behind
- **fix :** difficult or embarrassing situation; predicament

## What Does It Mean?

QUES...

1. My family practically disowned me.
2. His folks were more broad-minded about it.
3. a lifetime commitment



## Comprehension

QUES...

1. What do people think about unmarried couples living together?
2. What was the reason the woman began to live with her boyfriend before they got married?
3. When did they plan to marry?
4. How did her family react when they learned she was living with her boyfriend?
5. What did his family think about it?
6. After they lived together for a year, what did she find out?
7. Why is she thankful for not having married him?
8. Would she live with the next man she loves?
9. What does she think is the only way to get to know a potential spouse?

## Let's Talk!

1. Do you think living together before marriage is a good idea? Why or why not?
2. Why do some people have contempt for those who live together without being married?
3. What would you say if one of your children were going to live with someone of the opposite sex?
4. If a couple divorces, who do you think suffers more? The man or woman? Or, neither suffers more than the other?



## Opinion Samples

**1.** Strange to say, I now believe that couples who are serious about marriage should, at least, take a few weekend trips together to test their compatibility.

*(Q) What could you find about your future spouse if you took long trips together?*

**2.** A prenuptial agreement is an excellent idea for both parties should their marriage end in divorce. It does not necessarily mean that one doesn't trust the other. In a prenuptial agreement, you should be careful to protect your interest. This has nothing to do with trust or the lack of it. It's only common sense that any mutual agreement should be beneficial to all parties concerned.

*(Q) Would you recommend a prenuptial agreement to your children?*

→ **compatibility :** the ability of people or things to interact without problems
→ **prenuptial agreement :** consent, before marriage, of mutual rights, obligations and responsibilities in case of divorce

**3.** The best advice I ever received was a suggestion for a prenuptial agreement. The biggest mistake of my life was getting married without it. My recommendation: Insist on it. If a man and a woman can strike an equitable agreement in writing, they probably won't need to exercise it. If they can't reach an agreement, they'd better not get married.

*(Q) What would you do if your sweetheart refused to sign a prenuptial agreement?*

**4.** Albert Einstein once said, "You can't simultaneously prepare for and prevent war." So, to me, a prenuptial agreement seems like a vote of no confidence in advance of the wedding. How could anyone expect the marriage to work under those conditions?

*(Q) How can I decide if I should have a prenuptial agreement?*

**5.** Some people insist on "love at first sight," but I suggest that they calm down and take a second look. There is no such thing. Some of those attractive first-sight qualities may turn out to be genuine and durable, but don't count on the storybook formula.

The other bromide, "Love is blind," is far more sensible. The young girl (or an older one) who believes herself to be in love can't see the undesirable qualities in her man, because she wishes not to see them. To her, he is the most handsome, brightest, smoothest, sweetest, most adorable man in all the world. Perhaps his professor or his boss or his roommate may consider him irresponsible, ugly-tempered, lazy, or stupid, but she can't see any of this at all.

But no one can play a part forever. The mask must fall sooner or later. It is for this reason that I plead with people in love to live together for some time before they really get married.

*(Q) Do you believe in love at first sight? What does "Love is blind" mean?*

- **strike :** arrive at; achieve; confirm
- **equitable :** fair and impartial; just
- **simultaneous :** happening, existing, or done at the same time
- **quality :** personal trait, esp. one typical of overall character
- **count on :** rely on, depend on
- **storybook :** unreal, imaginary; falsely ideal
- **bromide :** meaningless saying or expression; platitude
- **mask :** (sth) that disguises or hides
- **plead :** appeal earnestly; beg

Issue 36

# Love or Selfishness?

Years ago, when my husband and I were first married, we discussed what would happen if one of us died.

We were both in our 30s at the time, so I didn't consider this a frivolous chat. We both promised never to remarry if one of us should pass away. I felt greatly relieved because I loved him so much I couldn't bear the thought of another woman taking my place.

We are now pushing 50, and I am seriously ill. Last night as we were sitting by the fireplace my husband brought up our old promise and assured me that it still stands. My question is this: Am I being unrealistic and selfish to find comfort in this promise? I don't think it would be too hard on him, because he's a workaholic anyhow and didn't marry me until he was in his mid-30s. We have no children and are devoted to each other. I can honestly say that if he died tomorrow I could easily live a purposeful life without ever having another man.

Are there other couples who have made this promise and been

- frivolous : not serious
- pass away : die
- pushing : approaching
- stand : remain in effect

able to keep it? Are there couples who made this promise and later regretted it? I am torn⁺ between the guilt I feel that I may be depriving him of years of future happiness and yet wanting so much to know that I will have been his only true love.

## What Does It Mean?

QUES...

1. I couldn't bear the thought of another woman taking my place.
2. He brought up our promise and assured me that it still stands.
3. I don't think it would be too hard on him.
4. purposeful life



## Comprehension

QUES...

1. What did this couple discuss when they got married?
2. Why didn't she think the discussion was frivolous?
3. What did they promise?
4. Was she relieved when her husband said the promise still stands? If so, why? If not, why not?
5. How old are they now?
6. Is she in good health? He?
7. Why does she think it would not be hard for him to keep his promise?
8. Why does she feel guilty?

→ **torn :** divided; greatly distressed

## Let's Talk!

1. Would you demand that your spouse not remarry when you died?
2. Could you promise your spouse not to remarry?
3. Even if people promise not to remarry after their spouse dies, many can't keep their word. Why not?
4. Is enforcing the promise an act of love or one of selfishness?
5. Which do you think is more important—one's promise or starting a new, happy life?
6. Would you want your sweetheart to remarry after you died?

## Opinion Samples

**1.** It seems to me that couples who truly love one another would want their mates to remarry. To exact a promise not to is the ultimate act of selfishness.

It is impossible to predict how one will feel several years down the road. People's ideas change. It would be extremely shortsighted to tie up a mate with such a promise, and I would definitely advise against it.

*(Q) If you were asked this question, would you be honest with your mate or lie?*

**2.** This kind of promise is easier made than honored. Even though people think they can keep the promise, as time goes by their determination can erode as feelings towards other people become stronger. Nobody can control another person's feelings. So it is very foolish to force such a promise.

*(Q) Do you think nobody can keep this kind of promise?*



- **exact :** insist on fulfillment of an agreement
- **down the road :** later on; in the future
- **shortsighted :** not thinking carefully about the possible effects of (sth) or what might happen in the future
- **against :** in opposition or resistance to
- **honored :** kept

Issue 37

# Lottery

I need an unbiased viewpoint. A friend I've known for 2 years moved near by. Since he was a close pal of long standing, I invited him to stay with me. We became roommates and got along fine.

We agreed that we would play the state lottery with the following understanding: Each of us would purchase at least one lottery ticket every week, and if any of those tickets were a winner we'd split the prize.

Although I was unemployed for a period of time and not eligible for unemployment benefits, I still managed to buy a ticket every week. Often when I asked my friend if he had bought his ticket he would say, "I forgot," or "The lines were too long."

Well, I hit five numbers, won $5,000, and decided not to cut him in on the money since I felt he had not kept his part of the agreement. Our lease was up and we parted. He has all but shut me out of his life and I'm sure this is the reason.

- **unbiased :** fair, not influenced by opinions, desires, etc.
- **split :** divide (sth) into two or more parts
- **eligible :** qualified or suited
- **lease :** long-term property rental, esp. of a house, apartment etc.
- **up :** finished; expired
- **all but :** almost
- **shut out :** closed; not associating with (sb)

## What Does It Mean?

1. close pal of long standing
2. not eligible for unemployment benefits
3. decided not to cut him in

## Comprehension

1. When they played the state lottery, what was their understanding?
2. Did the writer have a good job? What did he do?
3. Did his friend buy tickets every week as they promised? Explain your answer.
4. What were his excuses for not buying the tickets?
5. How many numbers did the writer hit and how much money did he win?
6. Why didn't he give some of the money to his friend, as he had agreed?

## Let's Talk!

1. Do you think he did the right thing?
2. What do you think about his friend's shutting the writer out of his life?
3. Can they make up? How? Should they?
4. Do you ever buy lottery tickets? Why or why not?
5. If you won a fortune, what would you do with the money?
6. Would you continue your job if you won the lottery?
7. What do you think about the government issuing lottery tickets to raise money instead of levying taxes?
8. People say you'll be poor 10 years after you win the lottery. Do you think that's true? Why or why not?

## Opinion Samples

**1.** The agreement was sloppy, to say the least. Too bad there wasn't anything in writing that invalidated the agreement under certain conditions. I would suggest that he give his friend $500, for friendship's sake, even though it could be argued that his friend wasn't entitled to anything.

*(Q) Would you take $500 if you were the friend? Would you insist on more, or not take anything at all?*

- **make up :** become friends again; be reconciled
- **issue :** circulate
- **levy :** impose or collect a tax
- **sloppy :** messy; not well organized
- **to say the least :** without exaggerating at all
- **invalidate :** make (sth) invalid or worthless
- **sake :** purpose
- **entitled :** rightfully deserving

**2.** He did nothing wrong. His friend didn't keep to the understanding, he just made lame excuses. He had no obligation to give anything to his friend.

*(Q) Do you think he is being selfish?*

**3.** At night I used to pretend that I had won a big jackpot, and then I would imagine all the things that would happen to me if I had a fortune.

My husband, who drinks too much, would quit his job and turn into a full-blown alcoholic. My teen-age children, who are unmotivated and need constant prodding, would drop out of school and loaf on a full-time basis. All my freeloading relatives (as well as my husband's) would be hitting on me to "help them out."

I would be inundated with letters from slick promoters with worthy causes and old friends with hard-luck stories. Suddenly I would be faced with big decisions, such as what kind of house to buy and what exclusive area I wanted to live in. Then I'd have to decide if I wanted a Mercedes or a Rolls-Royce.

After 15 minutes of envisioning my life as a millionaire I decided that I am better off with things the way they are.

*(Q) How can bad things happen if we win a lottery? How can this situation be avoided? Or is it unavoidable? Explain your response.*



- **understanding :** informal agreement
- **lame :** weak
- **jackpot :** the largest prize or award in a game or contest
- **full-blown :** fully developed
- **unmotivated :** without goals or purpose
- **drop out :** stop participating, as in a game, competition, or school
- **loaf :** do nothing; spend time lazily or aimlessly
- **free-load :** take free food and lodging, etc., without giving anything in return
- **hit on :** ask for favors
- **inundated :** overwhelmed
- **slick :** ingenious; clever
- **promoter :** organizer
- **cause :** idea or a goal to which one is absolutely dedicated
- **hard-luck :** unfortunate
- **envision :** imagine

**Issue 38**

# A Classic Mid-life Crisis

After working hard for 20 years, I have attained significant success in my field. Part of the reason was my husband's belief in my potential and his constant encouragement. Over the years, we celebrated my many promotions.

But recently, my husband filed for divorce. My friends called it "a classic mid-life crisis." (He just turned 40.) However, I believe the real reason for the divorce is my success.

Pop psychology "experts" have offered many glib explanations, but nothing can alleviate the pain I feel. I worked hard, became successful, and lost the man I love. Now I'm wondering if this is exclusively a male thing. I've never known a woman who divorced her husband because he became successful.

What do you think about this? Should I have seen it coming and slowed down? I love my career, but I also love him. Success is cold comfort in an empty bed.

- **classic :** well-known and typical
- **potential :** capacity for growth or development
- **pop :** popular; less than fully reliable
- **glib :** seemingly easy
- **alleviate :** make (sth) easier to bear; relieve; lessen
- **exclusive :** not shared with others

## What Does It Mean?

1. We celebrated my many promotions.
2. Pop psychology "experts" have offered many glib explanations.
3. exclusively a male thing
4. Should I have seen it coming and slowed down?
5. Success is cold comfort in an empty bed.



## Comprehension

1. How long did it take before she succeeded in her field?
2. How did her husband help her gain success?
3. Why does she think her husband filed for divorce?
4. What does she wonder about?
5. What does success mean to her?

## Let's Talk!

1. Are you for or against a wife having a career?
2. How would you feel if your wife made more money than you? What would you think about your husband if you made more money than he?
3. Would you help your wife with housework or child care if she had a job outside the home? Should a man be expected to do so?
4. Do you think it is true that a wife with a job tends to disregard her husband?
5. What factors lead many men to go through a mid-life crisis?
6. What's the difference between a crisis for a young person and one who is middle-aged?



disregard : pay little or no attention to

## Opinion Samples

**1.** This world is filled with women who are more successful than their husbands, and they are still married. There must have been other problems that she was not aware of.

The wise wife knows how to cut down the glare of the spotlight and move her husband closer to center stage. I wonder if she made an effort to do this. If so, there should be no self-recrimination. He would have left anyway.

*(Q) Do you think women become conceited if they make a lot of money?*

**2.** I don't understand her husband if there were no other problem except her successful career. Why should her success make him feel upset, jealous, or hurt? If he feels that way, it proves that he doesn't really love her. He needs to grow up.

*(Q) Some men become jealous of their wife's success while others welcome it. What's the main difference between these two kinds?*



- **glare :** dazzling light
- **recrimination :** accusation of bad conduct
- **grow up :** behave like an adult

Issue 39

# Search for Natural Parents

**[A]**

My parents separated when I was 4 years old. The divorce was very nasty, and I saw my father only a few times before he decided to move out of the state to avoid paying child support.

It wasn't until I became a father myself that I had a desire to see my dad again. I then read a letter in the newspaper stating that the Salvation Army locates* long-lost relatives. I saved that column, but waited for about five years before I wrote to the Salvation Army* about looking for my father.

To my great surprise, two months later the Salvation Army contacted me at my home, saying that they had found my dad and that he wanted to communicate with me! I was told that he was ill, so I hurriedly caught a plane and visited him in the hospital. I spent the weekend there, and we had a very nice time catching up on the 30-year gap in our relationship. Four days later, I received a call from the hospital, informing me that my father had just passed away!

In retrospect,* I suppose I should feel grateful for having had the chance to see my dad before he died. But in actuality, I agonized for a long time over the fact that I hadn't tried to find him sooner. I want to urge anyone who has a desire to locate a lost relative to do it today. Tomorrow may be too late.

**[B]**

You hear so much these days about adopted adults who want to find their "real" mothers. I may be unusual because I've never had any desire to find mine. My mother gave me up at birth for my own good—and hers. I'm grateful to her because the parents who raised me have given me a wonderful home.

I believe that most adopted adults who search for their

- **locate :** find (sb) or (sth) by searching or examining
- **Salvation Army :** charitable religious organization
- **in retrospect :** looking backward or reviewing the past

birth mothers must be unhappy with their lives. I feel sorry for parents who have adopted children and given them a good home, only to have them go looking for their "real" mothers. I would never do that.

So to all you adopted people, appreciate your good fortune and don't go poking around trying to find your "real" mother. The one you have couldn't be any more real.

## What Does It Mean?

1. The divorce was very nasty.
2. The Salvation Army locates long-lost relatives.
3. in retrospect
4. My mother gave me up at birth for my own good and hers.
5. Don't go poking around trying to find your "real" mother.

## Comprehension

**[A]** 1. When did the man's parents divorce?
2. Why did his father move out of the state?
3. When did the man get a desire to see his father?
4. Can you imagine why he waited another five years before he actually wrote the letter to the Salvation Army about locating his father? Why, do you think?
5. How long did it take for the Salvation Army to find his father?
6. Did he and his father have an argument? How did they spend their time together?
7. When did the father die?
8. Why should the man feel grateful?
9. Why was he also in agony?

**[B]** 1. Why does the writer think he is unusual?
2. Why is he grateful for his natural mother?
3. Does he believe that adopted adults should search for their natural parents? Explain your answer.

→ **poke around :** look for (sth), especially (sth) that is hidden

## Let's Talk!

1. Do you think it is natural for adopted adults to want to find their natural parents?
2. If you were an adopted adult, would you search for your natural parents?
3. If you had adopted children who wanted to get in touch with their natural parents, what would you tell them?
4. Do you think people are usually upset if their adopted children want to search for their natural parents?
5. Do you think adoption records should remain sealed unless the birth parents and the adopted children alike agree to opening them?
6. What are the reasons some people give up their babies for adoption?
7. Do you think any reasons are acceptable? Defend your answer.



sealed : permanently closed from view

## Opinion Samples

**1.** Many adopted adults desperately want to know about their roots, regardless of how wonderful their adoptive parents are. That is, after all, human instinct. If you were not interested in knowing about your natural mother, that might be okay for you, but remember—your real mother misses you a lot.

*(Q) Do you think you would want to meet your birth parents if you were adopted?*

**2.** Many adopted adults have no desire to find their birth parents, so they are not really unusual—but they are lucky not to worry about their own identity. And some birth mothers prefer not to be found, as is their right, due to shame or indifference.

*(Q) Why do some adopted adults have no desire to see their natural parents?*

**3.** Confidentiality in adoption should be guaranteed. Adoptees should be permitted to learn the medical history of their parents, out of their own self interest, but nothing more unless both the birth parents and the adopted child agree. Some matters are best left buried.

*(Q) Why do some birth parents refuse to see their own children after giving them up for adoption?*



- **roots :** ancestral connections
- **regardless of :** aside from
- **confidential :** secret; private
- **adoptee :** (sb) who is adopted

Issue 40

# Corporal Punishment

We should speak out against corporal punishment in our schools. Paddling kids with a board is itself child abuse, and it also promotes child abuse in our community by sending the message that it is OK for adults to hit children.

Paddling creates fear in children and lowers their self-esteem. This adds to the dropout rate and lowers test scores, since students naturally lose interest in being educated in a Nazi-like atmosphere. It also humiliates and angers children, thus increasing the vandalism and violence among youth.

Schools that forbid paddling are more peaceful, and the students appreciate being treated with respect. They respond in kind, by respecting their teachers and the school.

## What Does It Mean?

1. We should speak out against corporal punishment in our schools.
2. Nazi-like atmosphere

- **speak out :** publicly speak in protest about (sth)
- **paddling :** beating or spanking
- **vandalism :** intentional damage to or destruction of property

## Comprehension

QUES...

1. How does the writer think corporal punishment affects society?
2. How does paddling affect a child's psyche?
3. How does paddling affect children's school life?
4. What is the relationship between paddling and vandalism?

## Let's Talk!

1. Are you for or against paddling in school? Why?
2. What would you do if your child were paddled in school?
3. We often hear teachers say that they paddle their students entirely for the sake of the children's education. Do you really believe that? Or does paddling simply reflect the teacher's uncontrolled anger?
4. Do you spank your child at home? If so, when? If not, why not? (Conversely, have your parents ever paddled you?)
5. What are the side effects of corporal punishment?
6. Why do some teachers resort to paddling?
7. We hear teachers say that they have to paddle students in certain situations. Do you agree? Why or why not?
8. Who do you think is more responsible for a child's education, parents or teachers?



- **psyche :** soul or spirit; the human mind
- **resort to :** turn to for help, often as a final option

## Opinion Samples

**1.** We realize that in this age of one-parent households, latchkey children and increasing violence, we may feel we are losing control of the younger generation. That's partly because corporal punishment seems to have gone out of style, though in fact the principle never goes out of fashion. Children should be taught that violence causes more violence, and in that sense some degree of corporal punishment is necessary.

*(Q) What are the reasons today's children are becoming more violent?*

**2.** Children learn through example, and the message a child receives when he is struck, slapped, or paddled is that might makes right. So, all good lessons must come from the head and the heart—not the fist or the paddle.

Furthermore, teachers and principals should not be expected to do the parents' work. The job of the parent is to prepare a child for life, to make sure he gets a useful education, to teach him to respect his elders, and to guide him in his ability to work cooperatively with others.

*(Q) What are the different roles parents and teachers have in child education?*

**3.** I don't believe in hitting a child. A little slap on the wrist (just enough to hurt his dignity) is all right. However, hitting a child hard enough to hurt him physically may rid you of your hostilities, but it will only teach the child that violence is the answer to all conflicts.

*(Q) Instead of paddling children, what can be done to get them to behave properly?*

**4.** Parenting is a challenging, sometimes very difficult, job. When pressures build up, it is tempting to use physical punishment on a child. However, spanking a child in anger

- **latchkey child :** child who spends time alone at home after school
- **out of style :** out of fashion; not popular any longer
- **might :** physical strength
- **slap :** sharp blow with the open hand or some other flat object

can be dangerous, and children are often injured when an angry adult loses control.

*(Q) Have you ever taken your frustrations out on your children? If so, how did you feel afterwards?*

**5.** This society seems to value a "quick fix" to every problem; therefore, it is easier to hit a child than help him or her learn self-control. Children who are disciplined through constant hitting and spanking soon learn that the way to deal with life's frustration is to lash out at others physically.

Teaching children discipline is important. But the goal can be achieved without hitting or spanking. Children are more likely to do as we do than what we say. If parents want children to obey rules, to solve their own problems, to control their anger, and to live in peace with themselves and others, then the parents must set that example themselves.

*(Q) Do you think setting an example for children is easy?*



→ **lash out at :** attack (sb) violently
→ **set (an) example :** demonstrate a pattern or model, as of (sth) to be imitated or avoided

Issue 41

# When a Man Hits a Woman

I would like to explain why a woman might cause a man to become physically violent. I am in no way defending such masculine reactions. On the contrary, I am a nice guy who treats women with respect. Recently, however, I had an experience that made me understand quite clearly why a man might hit a woman.

Recently, a girl backed out of a date we had planned a week in advance. I had been eagerly looking forward to this occasion and had called during the week to confirm the time and place. I set aside the evening, saved the money I needed, cleaned out my car, and even got advice from female friends to make sure the evening was "perfect." I bought new clothes to wear and tried to look my best.

I showed up at the place we agreed to meet. She was 20 minutes late, and then when she arrived she told me our date was off because she already had a boyfriend and couldn't imagine why she had agreed to go out with me.

If a guy pulled that stunt, he would never get away with it. Such humiliation could result in violence. If more women were decent and fair, violent crimes against them wouldn't be so prevalent.

- **back out :** fail to keep a promise; withdraw from
- **in advance :** beforehand
- **off :** no longer in effect
- **pull (a) stunt :** do (sth) that is silly or slightly dangerous
- **prevalent :** widely existing or commonly occurring

## What Does It Mean?

1. in no way defending such actions
2. set aside the evening
3. make sure the evening was "perfect"
4. Our date was off.
5. If a guy pulled that stunt he would never get away with it.

## Comprehension

1. Does the writer defend male violence against women?
2. What did he do to prepare for his date?
3. When did his date appear? What did she say?
4. What does he think is the best way to prevent violence against women?



## Let's Talk!

1. Do you think violence against women can be justified in some cases? If so, when? If not, why not?
2. Why do men use violence against women?
3. What would you do if your husband hit you but repented immediately? Would you forgive him? Or would you seek a divorce?
4. People say it's never appropriate for a man to strike a woman. But what if she hits him first?
5. Would you marry a man who hit you during your courtship, thinking that you can change him after marriage?
6. Is there any way to deter men from beating their wives?
7. What do you think about verbal abuse between spouses?
8. Strange to say, there are many men who are hit by women. What do you think are some of the reasons? Why don't men defend themselves?

**courtship :** actively establishing a personal relationship that could lead to marriage

## Opinion Samples

**1.** What the woman did to him was lousy. But he described himself as a "nice guy who treats women with respect," even though he also said he can understand how some men might be pushed to the outer limits. This suggests to me that he is perfectly capable of doing just that. He sounds like a potential batterer to me.

*(Q) How can we know if someone is a potential batterer?*

**2.** Most men never stop at hitting once, even though they swear that they will never hit a woman again. If they hit their wife once, nine times out of ten they will be life-long batterers. How can we prevent this? The only answer to wife-beating is immediate divorce. Forgiving a batterer means giving him a license to commit violence again. Would-be wives must make it clear that under no circumstances will their husbands hit them. If they do not make their case very firmly, there is a high possibility that they will become victims of spousal violence.

*(Q) Is divorce the best solution to one spouse hitting the other?*

**3.** Many people comment that it is never okay for a man to hit a woman. I hope they will reconsider their stand. On numerous occasions I have seen women slap men. If anyone ever hit me, man or woman, I would not hesitate to hit that person back. That's how one gets respect.

Saying that hitting does not lead to genuine respect means nothing, it merely escalates the violence. No one has the right physically to abuse another person. Today's society needs to recognize that women can be just as abusive as men, and it is only fair that they be judged and punished the same way an abusive man would be.

*(Q) What would you do if your wife hit you?*



- **lousy :** mean, contemptible
- **pushed to the outer limits :** shoved to the edge of some situation
- **potential :** likely, possible
- **stand :** position

**4.** Researchers are finding that violence during courtship is as pervasive as violence within a marital relationship. Even more surprisingly, many individuals who are beaten, slapped, kicked, punched, and seriously injured with knives or guns go ahead and marry the abuser anyway.

Contrary to the popular belief that women are almost always the victims of domestic violence, one study showed no significant difference between the percentage of men and women engaged in life-threatening violence.

*(Q) Why do people put up with abusive behavior? What can they do about it?*

**5.** Why do men and women enter into abusive relationships? People tend to believe in the power of love to reform the loved one. Abusers have a number of traits in common, including a background of family violence, a low level of tolerance for stress, and zero self-esteem. A lack of religious belief is also a major factor. Violence may be also triggered by a variety of factors among couples who are dating. The major ones are jealousy, drinking and disagreements over children and housekeeping. Inability to control one's anger tops the lists as the main cause of violence. The inability to communicate is a close second.

Courtship, it seems, is a training ground for marriage. Unfortunately, it can also be a training ground for spousal abuse.

*(Q) Why do many people remain married to their abusers?*



- **pervasive :** present and perceived everywhere
- **domestic violence :** violence at home or in the family
- **abusive :** involving abuse or violence
- **trigger :** set off
- **top :** head

Issue 42

# Pro-life vs Pro-choice

This is a message to those who try to prevent women from entering abortion clinics and carry big signs that say, "They Kill Babies Here!"

Have any of you ever signed up to adopt a child? If not, why not? Is it because you don't want one, can't afford one, or don't have the time, patience, or desire to raise one?

What if a woman who was about to enter a family-planning clinic saw your sign and decided not to have an abortion after all but chose instead to give her baby up for adoption to you? Would you accept it? What if the mother belonged to a minority group—or was addicted to drugs or tested positive for AIDS?

Why are you spending your time carrying a sign? Why aren't you volunteering to baby-sit a child born to a single mother, so she can work? Why haven't you opened your door to a pregnant teen-ager whose parents kicked her out because she took your advice and decided not to have an abortion?

As for you taxpayers who resent paying for abortions, who do you think pays for foster care, welfare, social workers, and juvenile delinquency?

And let's talk about something money can't buy: love. Have you ever visited a home for abused and unwanted children? Have you ever been to court and seen all the children who commit crimes because they were born to mothers who didn't want them?

- **abortion :** the ending of a pregnancy
- **minority group :** group other than the majority or dominant group, esp. if socially discriminated against
- **addicted :** dependent on harmful, habit-forming substance
- **baby-sit :** take care of children in the temporary absence of the parents
- **foster care :** giving parental care to (sb) not legally related
- **juvenile delinquency :** antisocial or criminal behavior by non-adults

I'm not thrilled about abortion, but I don't think anyone has the right to tell others not to have one unless he has done all the things I mentioned above. Self-righteous hypocrisy does not solve any of the underlying problems.

## What Does It Mean?

1. tested positive
2. single mother
3. juvenile delinquency
4. not thrilled about abortion
5. If you are against abortion, don't be a hypocrite.

## Comprehension

1. Does the writer side with the pro-life or pro-choice movement?
2. According to the writer, what circumstances cause women to have abortions?
3. What does the writer want pro-life demonstrators to do?
4. Pro-life demonstrators grumble about tax money paid for abortions. Is this complaint logical?



- **hypocrisy :** the practice of showing or expressing feelings, beliefs, or virtues that one does not actually hold or possess
- **underlying :** basic; fundamental
- **side with :** support (sb/sth) in an argument, fight, etc.
- **grumble :** complain in a rude or unfriendly manner

## Let's Talk!

1. Do you think we must concede that an unborn baby has the same rights as any human being?
2. What's the difference between killing an unborn baby and killing a man in battle?
3. Is abortion an issue the government should intervene in, or something individuals must deal with by themselves?
4. Is it justifiable for pro-life people to kill abortion-performing doctors, calling them murderers?
5. Do you think a wife should have the right to have an abortion without the approval of the baby's father?
6. Are you mainly pro-life or pro-choice? Explain your reasons.

## Opinion Samples

**1.** The argument for abortion seems to hinge on the rights of women. But what about the rights of the children? If abortions are abolished, unwanted babies will be forced into the world, already grossly overcrowded and overburdened with problems that seem unsolvable. If the desire is to enforce morality, the criminalization of women's right to control their own body and the opposing of family planning are not the way to go about it.

*(Q) Is it logical to relate the abortion issue to overpopulation?*

**2.** Do you think it is fair that killing the already-born is murder, but killing unborn babies is not subject to criminal law? We all know that the right to life begins at conception, don't we?

*(Q) Do you think the unborn baby has the same right as any other human?*

---

- **concede :** admit (sth) as true or real, often unwillingly or hesitantly; acknowledge
- **intervene :** come between people in conflict order to help them reach an agreement
- **hinge on :** depend on
- **grossly :** extremely; exaggeratedly; not subtly or in a small way
- **subject to :** likely to be affected by

**3.** Above all, we should focus all our efforts on preventing unwanted pregnancy—through information, education, birth control, and affordable, available contraceptives. At the same time, we should also support a woman having the right to make her own decision concerning her own body. The decision should be primarily between a pregnant woman and her medical advisor. So I think the best policy is "Respect the right, but reduce the need."

*(Q) What do you think about men, and not just women, using contraceptives?*

**4.** If the church is really worried about saving the family and unborn children, why doesn't it offer to take all unwanted children under its wing and then either offer them up for adoption or raise them itself? It is of no use to show sympathy for unborn life and be against abortion without suggesting a practical solution.

*(Q) Who do you think should be responsible for taking care of unwanted babies?*

**5.** Pro-life groups do encourage information on birth control (not just abstinence) and sex education. They also promote the fact that all children, born and unborn, are precious—and all human life should be afforded the respect and dignity that it deserves.

*(Q) Do you think pro-life groups are too idealistic? That pro-choice advocates are too cynical?*



- **contraceptive :** a drug, object, or method used to make it possible for a woman to have sex without having a baby
- **under (its) wing :** within (its) protection or guidance
- **abstinence :** not allowing oneself to enjoy (sth)
- **cynical :** refusing to believe in goodness or honesty in people's actions

Issue 43

# Adoption

"Mom, I'm pregnant."
"You're WHAT?"
"I'm pregnant."
"This can't be true. Are you sure?"
"Yes, I've seen a doctor."
"What are you going to do about it?"
"I'm going to have the baby and put it up for adoption."
"You have no obligation to go through with this. We could arrange an abortion."
"I don't want an abortion. I'm going to have the baby."

We were sitting in a restaurant having dinner when this conversation took place. If anyone had told me that our daughter would get into this kind of mess, I would have questioned his sanity.

She was a college student, intelligent, a loving, all-around wonderful person. In my wildest dreams I never thought this would happen to her.

I told my husband. He had a difficult time accepting it too. Her sibling knew and was supportive. The next call was to her doctor. He confirmed everything and said she was in perfect health and would probably have a normal delivery. Then I telephoned an adoption agency. That was the most difficult part. An appointment was set up for our daughter and her father and me. I was afraid my husband would fold at the last moment, but he didn't.

We talked to a gentle and compassionate woman for over an hour. She assured us the baby would be placed in a loving home with parents who had been waiting for a child for many years. She made our daughter feel good about her decision and praised her mature judgment.

The ensuing months were a challenge. We gave our daughter a great deal of love and emotional support. The adoption agency provided excellent counseling to prepare her for the trauma ahead. We all went through the process of dealing with grief. The denial: "Was this really happening to us?" The guilt: "What did we do wrong?" The anger: "Why us?

- **obligation :** duty
- **sanity :** soundness of mind; good mental health
- **sibling :** brother or sister
- **delivery :** the act of giving birth
- **fold :** fail, fall, or collapse

So many young women do the same thing and get away with it." Out of the whole process came the acceptance of what we couldn't change.

The birth was a difficult one, but the baby was healthy, alert, and beautiful. I wept as I held my first grandchild in my arms. I knew she would not be mine for long and I dared not become too attached to her.

The new parents were ecstatic when they came to the hospital to claim "their" baby. There were many tears, hugs, and kisses as they left with their daughter in their arms. They promised to give her the best home ever, and I'm sure they will keep their word.

Our daughter is back in college, making excellent grades, and is happy and well-adjusted. I now understand why she could never consider abortion. Why didn't I think of it before? It should have been obvious. She herself is an adopted child.



## What Does It Mean?

1. in my wildest dreams
2. I was afraid my husband would fold at the last moment.
3. The ensuing months were a challenge.
4. trauma ahead
5. dared not become too attached

## Comprehension

1. Where were they when the conversation took place?
2. What were they talking about?
3. What did the woman suggest to her daughter?
4. Did the daughter want to have an abortion?
5. When the father was notified about the pregnancy, how did he feel?
6. What did various people do during the ensuing months?
7. Was the birth easy?
8. Describe the baby.
9. What is the daughter doing now?
10. Why does the mother think the daughter put the baby up for adoption instead of having an abortion?

**ecstatic :** feeling extremely happy and excited

**keep (one's) word :** do as promised

## Let's Talk!

1. If you were medically unable to have a baby, would you adopt one?
2. If you were too poor to take care of your new-born baby, would you give him up so he could have a better life?
3. Do you think that giving up a baby for adoption, especially just so he could have a better living standard, is morally acceptable?
4. If the natural mother changes her mind and decides later to get her baby back, who do you think has the superior right to take care of the child, the natural mother or the adoptive one?
5. Do you think there is any difference between raising your own babies and adopted ones?
6. What problems can you imagine occurring if you were to bring up your own child and an adopted one at the same time?
7. Should parents tell their adopted children about the true circumstances of their birth?

## Opinion Samples

**1.** I would never give up my baby for adoption under any circumstances. Many mothers think that it can be justified because their children could then be brought up in a financially better-off family. But nothing is more important to the baby than to be brought up by its natural parents. To me, giving up a baby for adoption can never be suitable, and especially not for some paltry economic advantage.

*(Q) What if the natural parents are too poor to take care of children adequately? Would adoption be in the child's best interests?*

- **justify :** show or prove (sb) or (sth) to be right, just, or valid
- **paltry :** of little worth or importance

**2.** If you became pregnant and were not in a position to take proper care of the baby, what should you do? The best alternative is to apply for adoption. Adoptive parents are carefully screened for eligibility. In general, they tend to be financially well off, and there is no reason to believe that they can't be good parents.

*(Q) What are some of the most important qualifications for adoptive parents?*

**3.** I am 42 years old. My husband and I have been trying to conceive for eight years. We are both successful professionals. We have a beautiful home and no money problems, and would make wonderful, loving parents. We have been on the waiting lists of three adoption agencies for two years and keep praying that one of them will call us with great news.

If you are not able to take care of your baby, contact an agency through your clergyman or your doctor and ask that the child be placed with a loving couple whose empty arms long to hold a little one. You will be rewarded for this act of generosity and feel good in your heart, forever knowing you have done the right thing.

*(Q) Why do people want to have children?*



- **alternative :** choice
- **eligibility :** qualification; suitability

Issue 44

# To Remember Me

The day will come when my body will lie upon a white sheet neatly tucked under four corners of a mattress in a hospital busily occupied with the living and the dying. At a certain moment, a doctor will determine that my brain has ceased to function and that, for all intents and purposes, my life has stopped.

When that happens, do not attempt to instill artificial life by the use of a machine. And don't call this my deathbed. Let it be called the Bed of Life, and let my body be taken from it to help others lead fuller lives.

Give my sight to the man who has never seen a sunrise, a baby's face or love in the eyes of a woman. Give my heart to a person whose own heart has caused nothing but endless days of pain. Give my blood to the teenager who was pulled from the wreckage of his car, so that he might live to see his grandchildren play. Give my kidneys to one who depends on a machine to exist. Take my bones, every muscle, every fiber and nerve in my body and find a way to make a crippled child walk.

Explore every corner of my brain. Take my cells, if necessary, and let them grow so that, someday, a speechless boy will shout at the crack of a bat and a deaf girl will hear the sound of rain against her window.

Burn what is left of me and scatter the ashes to the winds to help the flowers grow.

If you must bury something, let it be my faults, my

- **tuck :** gather and fold (sth) under
- **instill :** implant
- **crack :** sharp snapping sound

weakness and all prejudice against my fellow man. If, by chance, you wish to remember me, do it with a kind deed or word to someone who needs you. If you do all I have asked, I will live forever.

## What Does It Mean?

1. for all intents and purposes
2. instill artificial life by the use of a machine
3. who depends on a machine to exist

## Comprehension

1. Does the writer want to prolong life artificially?
2. Why does the writer want to call his deathbed the Bed of Life?

## Let's Talk!

1. What do you think about organ donation?
2. Do you carry an organ donation card?
3. If your child were declared brain-dead, would you donate his or her usable organs to some stranger in need?
4. What do you think about your body being donated to medical research after you die?
5. What's the difference between donating some organ while you're alive (such as a kidney), and donating your entire body when you are dead?

## Opinion Samples

**1.** Some people think it is "just wonderful" that a family donates the body of the deceased to be cut up and given to people who need a new lung, a new heart, new eyes, new kidneys, etc. And the skin, to be used by someone who has been badly burned.

But I find it incredible that they can conceive of cutting a body to pieces as "an act of enormous generosity." To me, it is just plain gruesome. If my son were killed in an accident, I would never allow his body to be cut up for any reason whatsoever. I would want the world to know that I loved and respected him in death as in life, and I would see to it that he was lain to rest in a dignified manner.

Where the hell do these people get off advising people to desecrate a loved one's remains? It is just a twisted form of do-goodism.

- **gruesome :** causing horror and shock; frightful
- **see to it that :** make sure that
- **the hell :** used to emphasize a speaker's denial or disagreement
- **where . . . get off :** How . . . have the attitude of
- **desecrate :** damage (sth) sacred
- **remains :** corpse
- **twisted :** not normal; weird
- **do-goodism :** actions or principles of a well-intentioned but naive person

*(Q) Do you think the writer would maintain his point of view if he or his child urgently needed an organ to save his life?*

**2.** Let us assume for a minute that your son was suddenly stricken blind, and the doctors told you his sight could be restored by a corneal transplant. Would you not thank God for the miracle of modern medicine and be enormously grateful to the family that agreed to donate their dead child's eyes so that your child could see?

*(Q) Selling organs is against the law. What would happen if it became legal?*

**3.** Only organ recipients know that the need for organ donation is enormous and there is no gift as great as this one. Organ recipients are deeply indebted to a family they will never know. Organ donation turns a sad loss for one family into tremendous joy for another. What better way is there to immortalize a loved one than by giving new life to others? There are many people waiting for this medical miracle. Signing a donor card and making your wishes known to others is easy, and it is a gift beyond measure.

*(Q) Can you imagine how organ recipients must feel?*



- **indebted :** owing another person money or gratitude for a loan, gift, or useful service
- **immortalize :** prevent (sb) or (sth) from dying or being forgotten
- **beyond measure :** impossible to determine exactly

Issue 45

# Sex Appeal

I am in my mid-40s, still attractive, and know that the odds of finding a partner drop tremendously at my age. I'm engaged to a man that I'm not "in love" with. I admire, respect, and like him—as a friend. We have a lot of fun together, and the companionship is great. He supports me in my career and accepts me exactly as I am. He's handsome and treats me like a queen, but there is no chemistry between us.

I've been married before and I have also been in relationships where incredible electricity flowed, but one of them turned out to be the most personally destructive situation I've ever been in. (He was handsome, charismatic, and abusive.) I have come to the conclusion that intensity often characterizes sick relationships and I won't get into another one if I can avoid it. But I also know I'm missing that wonderful feeling of being in love.

- **odds :** likelihood or probability that (sth) will happen
- **chemistry :** sexual attraction
- **charisma :** having the exceptional ability to lead and win the devotion of large numbers of people

## What Does It Mean?

1. There is no chemistry.
2. Incredible electricity flowed.

## Comprehension

1. How old is the writer?
2. Does she think she can easily find a lover at her age?
3. Does she love her fiance?
4. What is her fiance like?
5. Does she hate relationships based primarily on sex appeal?
6. Describe her most memorable relationship.

## Let's Talk!

1. Do you think sex appeal should be an important factor in marriage? Why or why not?
2. Who would you rather choose to marry, someone with sex appeal or a socially successful person without much sexual attraction?
3. What is the difference between love and infatuation?
4. Do you think sex appeal is important on the job market? Why or why not?
5. Do you think sex appeal fades as time goes by?



## Opinion Samples

**1.** Although it is not necessarily true that intensity characterizes "sick" relationships, the intensity seldom lasts in any relationship. Her fiance sounds like a first-class "catch." It depends on how important "the sparks" are. Some women could never settle for a relationship that wasn't sexually exciting, while others place a much higher premium on kindness, compatibility, good character, and reliability.

*(Q) What do you think is the most important factor in a relationship?*

**2.** Infatuation is instant desire. Love is a friendship that has caught fire. It takes root and grows, one day at a time.

Infatuation is marked by a feeling of insecurity. You are excited and eager but not genuinely happy. There are nagging doubts, unanswered questions, little bits and pieces about your beloved that you would just as soon not examine too closely. It might spoil the dream. Love is the quiet understanding and mature acceptance of imperfection. It is real. It gives you strength and grows beyond you—to bolster your beloved. You are warmed by his presence, even when he is away. Miles do not separate you. You want him near. But near or far, you know he is yours and you know you can wait until he returns.

Infatuation says, "We must get married right away. I can't risk losing him." Love says, "Be patient. He is yours. Plan your future with confidence." Infatuation has an element of sexual excitement. Whenever you are in one another's company you hope it will end in intimacy. Love is the maturation of friendship. You must be friends before you can be lovers.

Infatuation lacks confidence. When he's away you wonder if he's cheating. Sometimes you check up on him. Love means trust. You are calm, secure and unthreatened. He feels your trust, and it makes him even more trustworthy. Infatuation might lead you to things you'll regret later, but love never will.

Love lifts you up. It makes you look up. It makes you a better person than you were before.

*(Q) Do you think the difference is always clear between love and infatuation?*



- **infatuation :** very strong feelings of love or attraction for (sb) or (sth), especially when these are unreasonable and do not last long
- **bits and pieces :** small things of various kinds
- **bolster :** support or reinforce
- **beloved :** (sb) who is dearly loved
- **intimacy :** personal closeness in a relationship; sex
- **maturation :** the process of growing or developing
- **lift (sb) up :** make (sb) feel more cheerful and more hopeful

Issue 46

# Is Money a Proper Gift?

When my niece graduated from college recently, I asked her mother for some gift suggestions. I was told, "She wants money."

When we received a wedding invitation from a couple we watched grow up, I called both mothers and asked if there was something special that we might buy them. I got the same response, "They want money."

Don't these people realize that the purpose of the gift is to commemorate an important milestone in their lives? I wanted to give the young couple something they would treasure forever.

Am I hopelessly out of date? I have always felt that cash is what you give when you don't want to bother with shopping. Writing a check is a great deal easier than going from store to store looking for the gift that is just right.

I refuse to give money and I resent being asked to help pay for a yuppie's Caribbean honeymoon.

- **commemorate :** honor the memory of (sb or sth)
- **milestone :** significant or important event
- **out of date :** old-fashioned, outmoded
- **yuppie :** young, ambitious, educated city dweller with a high-paying profession and a prosperous lifestyle; insulting term for a materialistic person

## What Does It Mean?

1. Am I hopelessly out of date?
2. Cash is what you give when you don't want to bother with shopping.
3. I resent being asked to help pay for a yuppie's Caribbean honeymoon.

## Comprehension

1. What does the writer think is the purpose of a gift?
2. What kind of present does the writer want to give?
3. When do people give cash as a gift, according to the writer?
4. What does the writer resent?

## Let's Talk!

1. What do you think about giving cash as a gift?
2. When do you give a cash present?
3. Why do some people think cash is not a proper gift?
4. Why do some people think cash is the best gift?

## More Talking Points

**What kind of present do you think is appropriate for the following?**

(a) Wedding anniversary (for your spouse)
(b) Birthday (for a friend/for your child/for your lover/for your elderly parents)
(c) Your child's graduation
(d) Your spouse's promotion.

## Opinion Samples

**1.** I think the writer's view is direct and to the point. Money is an appropriate gift from parents or grandparents, but to suggest that other family members or friends write a check is crass.

*(Q) Why is it strange to ask others to give cash gifts while monetary presents from parents and grandparents are okay?*

**2.** The reason I don't want to give cash is that if I give people money and they spend it, then they forget my celebrating their special occasion. But if I give them some special gift, they cannot forget me as long as they keep it.

*(Q) Agree or disagree?*

crass : offensive, unfeeling

**3.** When my birthday comes along, a gift of cash looks good to me, an elderly woman. I defend gifts of cash. I am on Social Security, and when I get through the monthly bills, and the various holiday, birthday, graduation, shower and wedding gifts, I have no money left. I want to cry when I answer a knock on my door and see a messenger with one of those floral arrangements, which will be dead in a week. I can't eat it, wear it, or even find room for it in my tiny apartment. Adding to our worldly goods is more a burden than a blessing.

We senior citizens have plenty of time to shop, we adore bargains, and we don't need any necklaces, sexy nightgowns, perfumes or even magazine subscriptions.

I'd rather have a dollar bill than a useless gift worth 10 times that amount.

*(Q) Why do elderly people want cash gifts?*

**4.** My son is getting married in six months to a lady who also has a fully equipped house. How can we suggest to their wedding guests that they need almost nothing, but are planning a tour to Europe next year, and cash gifts toward their trip would be very much appreciated?

I think it's sinful that so many gifts are inappropriate, some are duplicates, and so much time is spent shopping and wrapping, while the gifts themselves go into a closet, eventually to be used as gifts for someone else!

We should start a campaign to make checks socially acceptable as wedding gifts.

*(Q) Is the writer realistic? Or is it an insult to ask for cash gifts from friends and relatives, especially for a wedding?*

- **defend :** support or maintain (sb) or (sth), as by argument; justify
- **Social Security :** government subsidy to the elderly, unemployed, or disabled
- **get through :** finish
- **worldly :** relating to material things
- **subscription :** advance order to buy (sth), such as issues of a magazine
- **sinful :** very bad; seriously wrong; shameful
- **duplicate :** exact copy
- **eventually :** ultimately
- **check :** written order directing a bank to pay money

Issue 47

# *Every Man for Himself?*

The order to abandon ship automatically presupposes two rules: Women and children go first, and the captain is the last to leave or goes down with his vessel. Romanticized by novels and films as well as history, the maxim seems to have almost the force of law. Thus, though all 571 people aboard the Greek cruise liner Oceanos survived its spectacular sinking off the coast of South Africa recently, the ship's captain, Yiannis Avranas, was widely castigated as being cowardly and irresponsible. Avranas, 51, left the Oceanos aboard a rescue helicopter while some 160 passengers, including several elderly and infirm, still awaited evacuation. He abdicated the hero's role to a South African entertainer, who not only operated the shipboard radio and made certain everyone was safe but also rescued Avranas' own dog and released the captain's pet canary from its cage, before becoming one of the last to quit the sinking vessel.

In reality there is no law of the sea that requires the captain to remain with his ship to the end. And Avranas, backed by his employers, argued that with communications on board so bad, the evacuation was best directed from shore. But the captain's statements immediately after the disaster did not help his popular standing. "When I order abandon ship, it doesn't matter what time I leave," he said. "If some people want to stay longer, they can."

- **abandon ship :** leave a ship because it is sinking
- **presuppose :** take for granted in advance
- **castigate :** reprimand or criticize severely
- **cowardly :** behaving in a way that shows that you are not brave
- **infirm :** feeble or weak
- **evacuate :** leave an area due to an emergency
- **abdicate :** give up power or responsibility formally
- **quit :** leave or depart from a place
- **backed :** supported

## What Does It Mean?

1. Romanticized by novels and films as well as history, the maxim seems to have almost the force of law.
2. But the captain's statements immediately after the disaster did not help his popular standing.

## Comprehension

1. What are the two conventional rules when a ship is to be abandoned?
2. What happened to the Greek cruise liner Oceanos?
3. What did the ship's captain do?
4. To whom did the captain give up his hero's role?
5. Is there a law that forces the captain to give up his life with his ship?
6. Did the employers criticize the captain?
7. What did he say when he tried to justify himself?

## Let's Talk!

1. Do you think the conventional rule that requires the captain to leave the ship last is fair?
2. Do you think Captain Avranas deserves criticism?
3. What would you do if you were the captain of a sinking ship?
4. Who should leave a sinking ship first? Why?



deserve : be worthy of (sth)

## Opinion Samples

**1.** The traditional rules must be observed, even if not enforced by law. That is the only hope for the people aboard if they are faced with an emergency. If it were nothing but empty rhetoric, no one would believe in the ship's safety or crew's morality. And no captain could maintain his authority in an emergency situation, which could result in even more casualties.

*(Q) Would you die with your sinking ship if you were a captain?*

**2.** This is about a man's life, not a romantic feeling. No one can force a captain to do "unnecessary" brave actions and risk his life. If he performs his duties as required in an emergency, he should not be under any criticism. All lives are equally important.

*(Q) If a captain enjoys the privileges of his position, shouldn't he also accept its responsibilities?*



- **emergency :** serious situation that happens suddenly or unexpectedly and calls for immediate action
- **empty rhetoric :** words without conviction or accompanying action
- **crew :** people working together to operate a ship, plane, spacecraft, or train
- **authority :** the power to enforce laws, command obedience, or judge
- **casualties :** those killed or injured in an accident or a military action

Issue 48

# Childless Couple

There is nothing sadder than a childless couple. It breaks one's heart to see them stretched out, relaxing around a swimming pool in Florida or California, suntanned and miserable on the deck of a boat, trotting off to enjoy Europe like lonesome fools—with money to spend, time to enjoy themselves and nothing to worry about. Childless couples become so selfish and wrapped up in their own concerns, one can't help but feel sorry for them.

Everyone should have children. No one should be allowed to escape the wonderful experiences attached to each stage in the development of the young. The happy memories of those early years: saturated mattresses, waiting for sitters who don't show up, midnight asthma attacks, rushing to the hospital emergency room to get the kid's head stitched up.

Children are worth every moment of anxiety, every sacrifice. You knew it the first time you took your son hunting. He didn't mean to shoot you in the leg. Remember how he cried? How sorry he was? How disappointed you weren't a deer? These are the memories a man treasures forever.

Think back to that night of romantic adventure when your budding, beautiful daughter eloped with the village

- **stretch out :** lie down, usually in order to sleep or rest
- **suntanned :** being dark as a result of exposure to the sun
- **trot off :** go at a quick, steady pace; move briskly; hurry
- **saturated :** thoroughly wet
- **sitter :** (sb) who cares for children when the parents are not home
- **asthma :** lung disease that causes tightness of the chest, coughing, and difficulty breathing
- **emergency room :** section of a hospital intended to provide rapid treatment for victims of sudden illness or trauma
- **stitch :** sew
- **treasure :** value highly; cherish
- **budding :** beginning to develop
- **elope :** run away with a lover to get married, without parental consent or knowledge

idiot. What childless couple can ever share in such a wonderful growing experience? Could a woman without children have the strength and heroism of your wife when she tried to fling herself out of the bedroom window? Only a father could have the courage to stand by, ready to jump after her.

The emptiness of life without children is indescribable. Childless couples live in a vacuum. They try to fill their lonely lives with dinner dates, theater, golf, tennis, swimming, civic affairs and trips all over the world.

See what the years have done. He looks boyish, unlined and rested. She is slim, well-groomed and youthful. It isn't natural. If they had kids, they'd look like the rest of us—tired, gray, wrinkled and haggard. In other words, normal.



## What Does It Mean?

QUES...

1. wrapped up in their own concerns
2. No one should be allowed to escape the wonderful experiences attached to each stage in the development of the young.
3. Children are worth every moment of anxiety, every sacrifice.
4. These are the memories a man treasures forever.
5. when your budding, beautiful daughter eloped with the village idiot
6. Childless couples live in a vacuum.
7. The emptiness of life without children is indescribable.
8. She is slim, well-groomed and youthful.

- **fling :** throw
- **stand by :** be ready or available to act
- **boyish :** looking or behaving like a boy
- **unlined :** not wrinkled
- **well-groomed :** looking clean, neat and carefully dressed
- **haggard :** appearing worn and exhausted

## Comprehension

1. What does the writer think about childless couples? Is he being serious or ironic?
2. Why does the writer think childless couples are selfish?
3. What are some of the wonderful experiences in bringing up children?
4. What do childless couples do to fill their loneliness?
5. If people have kids, how do they physically change as time goes by?



## Let's Talk!

1. Why do so many people want children?
2. Talk about the reasons some people don't want children.
3. How many children do you want to have?
4. If you had some difficulty in having babies, would you want to adopt?
5. We have an old saying, "Being childless is the best option." What do you think is the real meaning of this?
6. What does having a boy mean to you?
7. What does having a girl mean to you?
8. Is there any difference in bringing up boys and girls?
9. Is there any difference in attitude between childless adults and those with children?

## Opinion Samples

**1.** Don't assume that the decision not to have children is mainly due to an emotional deficiency resulting from a lack of affection from parents.

Why must people assume there is something wrong with people who choose to be childless? Does someone have to be a little off in order to make this choice? Is someone a cold fish simply because he or she doesn't want kids? Nonsense.

Even though people are childless, they may be perfectly normal and quite content with their lives. And, without the need to take care of their children, they can enjoy spending their leisure time with one another.

*(Q) Are childless people selfish? Why or why not?*

**2.** If I hadn't had children, I would probably have had more money and material things. I probably would have been to more places, gotten more sleep and pampered myself more.

But my life would have been more boring and predictable. As a result of being a parent, I have laughed harder and cried more often. I have worried more and hurried more. I've had less sleep, but somehow I've had more fun. I've learned more and grown more. My heart has ached harder, and I've loved to a capacity beyond my imagination. I've given more of myself, but I've derived more meaning from life.

*(Q) What do children mean in our lives?*



- **assume :** take (sth) for granted; suppose
- **emotional deficiency :** lacking in feeling
- **off :** crazy; eccentric
- **cold fish :** (sb) who lacks emotional warmth, compassion, or sociability; aloof person
- **content :** satisfied
- **pamper :** treat with too much kindness or care
- **capacity :** limit
- **derive :** obtain or receive

**3.** I believe many people have kids in order to appear "normal". Others are afraid of being lonely when they get on in years. Still others need something to brag about.

Parenthood is an enormous responsibility. Being a parent means headaches and heartaches. Furthermore, there are no guarantees that children will bring happiness.

Some people do not make suitable parents because they are unwilling to make sacrifices, which involve loss of personal freedom, to say nothing of the money it takes to raise kids. I admit I don't want children, for all the reasons I've mentioned. But I'm a little afraid people will consider me a freak if I never have any.

*(Q) Talk about the advantages and disadvantages of being childless.*

**4.** It is no longer a "sin" not to want children. Our planet has become overpopulated, polluted, drug-crazy and crime-ridden. No matter where you look, there is a war someplace. No reason to bring children into a world like this.

*(Q) Is the decision to remain childless for the sake of the couple or of the children?*

**5.** You're obligated to have kids, because your parents had you. You don't know what you're missing. Kids can bring enormous pleasure and may be the best part of your life.

*(Q) Do you agree that kids are gifts from God?*

---

- **get on in years :** grow old
- **brag :** boast
- **make :** become
- **to say nothing of :** without need to mention
- **freak :** abnormal, unusual, or strange person
- **our planet :** Earth
- **drug-crazy :** made insane by drugs
- **crime-ridden :** full of criminal actions
- **obligated :** forced, required

**6.** It is very easy to cast judgment on others, but I suggest you "walk in their shoes." The saddest part of my day is when I hear the endless complaints some people make about their children. This is the injustice of it all: They are blessed with gifts from God—their children—yet do nothing but complain of the responsibility, cost, problems, etc. They may well just be raising children who in turn will be childless by choice because of their parents' attitude.

*(Q) Many people complain about their children. Do you think they really regret having kids?*



- **cast judgment :** judge
- **walk in (one's) shoes :** be in, or imagine to be in, another person's situation
- **choice :** voluntary decision; free will

Issue 49

# Gender Favoritism

**[A]**

I am in my seventh month of pregnancy, but because of my husband's attitude I feel as if I have been carrying this baby for a year. He has shot off his big mouth to everyone who will listen that if I don't have a boy he will leave us both in the hospital.

Everyone laughs it off, and so do I, but it really does hurt. If I have a girl, I will feel as if I have failed him. To make matters worse, his two brothers' wives have had three girls apiece, and they say they are "through." I am afraid my in-laws are counting on me to have a son, although they have been gracious enough to say it doesn't matter.

**[B]**

My parents and I have a very poor relationship. They've seen my 5-month-old daughter only three times. I have an older sister and two brothers. We all live in the same city.

The favoritism shown to our brothers has caused my sister and me a lot of pain. This has been going on for as long as we can remember. In our last phone conversation, I came right out and told my mother that I still hurt from the emotional abuse I have suffered since early childhood, and that her favoritism towards "the boys" is very painful. I asked, point blank, why she did this to my sister and me. There was no answer.

The reason I felt compelled to be so blunt was because I had had a serious illness several weeks before and my parents had not bothered to visit me in the hospital or send a card. I was crushed by this ultimate rejection.

Can it be that some parents just don't want daughters? My sister is a wonderful person and everyone loves her. It has taken me a long time to see that I, too, am lovable and have many friends.

I have two precious daughters and it boggles my mind that parents would not value their granddaughters.

- **shoot off (one's) big mouth :** boast; talk to vehemently
- **fail :** disappoint
- **through :** finished; no longer effective or able
- **crush :** destroy
- **boggle the mind :** amaze

## What Does It Mean?

1. He has shot off his big mouth to everyone.
2. Everyone laughs it off.
3. If I have a girl, I will feel as if I have failed him.
4. They say they are "through".
5. My in-laws are counting on me to have a son.
6. I came right out.
7. point blank
8. My parents had not bothered to visit me in the hospital or send a card.
9. I was crushed by this ultimate rejection.
10. It boggles my mind that parents would not value their granddaughters.



## Comprehension

**[A]** 1. What did the husband say he would do if his wife doesn't have a boy?
2. Did anyone take his statement seriously?
3. How many girls do his two brothers have?
4. Will they try to have a boy again?
5. Do her parents-in-law say they count on her to have a son?

**[B]** 1. Why does the woman have a poor relationship with her parents?
2. What did her mother say when asked why she favors her sons over her daughters?
3. Did her parents visit her when she was in the hospital? How did that make her feel?

## Let's Talk!

1. How many children do you want to have?
2. Do you want boys or girls?
3. If your spouse did not want to have daughters, what would you do?
4. What are the reasons people generally favor boys over girls?
5. Would you want to live with your son after he gets married? Why or why not?

## Opinion Samples

**1.** These clatter traps who specify a preference are a strange breed of jackass, and there is no known cure. If her husband were the king of Siam, he might have a succession problem. But since he's not, what's his beef? Husbands who advertise they want sons always wind up nutty as fruitcakes over their daughters. It never fails.

*(Q) What's the difference between raising boys and girls?*

**2.** Her mother sounds seriously disturbed and probably also came from a dysfunctional family. It is possible that she had a very poor relationship with her own mother, and there hangs the whole sad tale.

*(Q) Who favors boys more, men or women?*



- **clatter trap :** bigmouth; foolishly over-talkative person
- **jackass :** very foolish or stupid person; blockhead; dolt
- **beef :** complaint
- **wind up :** end up; finish
- **nutty as fruitcakes :** completely crazy
- **dysfunctional :** not following the normal patterns of social behavior
- **hang :** attach; depend; explain

Issue 50

# Divorce

Once upon a time, there was a bright young man who wanted to become rich and successful. So he studied very hard in college, got an M.B.A., and went to work in a prestigious firm.

Since most successful businessmen in the land had beautiful wives, he went out and got himself one, too. He bought her a lovely home in the suburbs. In return for beautiful clothes and elegant jewels, she was a dutiful wife who devoted herself to their children. She never saw much of her rich, successful husband, who worked long hours and stayed out late at night, sharing wine and expensive meals with potential clients in order to cultivate good connections. There were also rumors that he was seen dining with attractive women in the business world.

Meanwhile, his wife was growing more lonely and disconnected, day by day. Finally, after looking at the emptiness of her life, she decided to go back to college and find a career. After watching her husband, she knew she didn't want to be rich and successful. She was hungry for something much deeper and more meaningful.

Something inside her awakened as she gained new knowledge. And, one day in class, her eyes locked with those of a handsome man who was also looking for something that would give meaning to his life. He was tired of the demands of the business world, and wanted true happiness and satisfaction.

After a year of contemplation, she divorced her husband (who to this day remains baffled but busy) and married the nice man in her class. He became a good stepfather to her

- **MBA :** Master of Business Administration (academic degree)
- **prestigious :** highly regarded; respected; esteemed
- **contemplation :** looking at or thinking about (sth) thoroughly
- **baffled :** confused
- **stepfather :** the husband of one's mother by a later marriage

children, who were delighted to have a man to spend time with, and he always came home from work in time for the family dinner. They weren't rich, but they lived happily ever after.

## What Does It Mean?

1. potential clients
2. cultivate good connections
3. growing more lonely and disconnected
4. looking at the emptiness of her life
5. hungry for something much deeper and more meaningful
6. tired of the demands of the business world



## Comprehension

1. What did the wife do in return for the beautiful clothes and elegant jewels?
2. Did she and her husband often enjoy themselves together? Why or why not?
3. While she was alone at home, what did her husband do?
4. After examining her life, what did she want?
5. How long did she contemplate a divorce?
6. How did her children feel about their new father?

## Let's Talk!

1. Do you ever think of getting a divorce? Talk about situations in which you might consider one.
2. Why are people reluctant to file for divorce, even if they feel they have to?
3. Who is in a better position to take care of their children after a divorce, the mother or the father?
4. If your spouse had a love affair, would you get divorced or forgive the transgression? Or get even by having an affair of your own?
5. How could you tell if your spouse were having an affair?
6. How can society reduce the divorce rate?
7. If one of your family members or friends were getting a divorce, would you simply "butt out" or try to help save the marriage?
8. Who do you think should usually get child custody, the mom or the dad? What do you think should determine the issue?
9. It is said that many husbands and wives refuse to take care of their own children when divorced. Why is that?

## Opinion Samples

**1.** It is true that divorces are too easy to get. But the real problem is that it is too easy to get married. I don't understand why so many people are in such a hurry. Are they afraid that if they don't get wedded at once, the "fish" will get away? I think if love is here to stay, it will be here today, tomorrow, next week, next month or even next year.

If people took a little more time to get to know each other before they married, there wouldn't be so many divorces. There should be a law that makes it mandatory to be officially engaged for at least six months. That means a couple should apply for a marriage license, and if they are still

- **transgression :** violation (of a law, for ex.)
- **butt out :** not interfere
- **child custody :** legal right to care for a child or children
- **mandatory :** required; obligatory
- **engaged :** promised to be married

together six months later they would be allowed to get married. This would certainly do a lot to knock down the horrendous number of divorces. I'm speaking from experience. If I had had to wait six more months, I would never have gotten married and would have avoided a very nasty divorce.

*(Q) How can a long engagement help reduce the divorce rate?*

**2.** My parents hated each other, but they stayed together because of their religious convictions. I wished every day of my childhood that they would get a divorce so we could have some peace.

They fought about anything and everything, and then they'd take it out on us kids. They never hit each other, but they beat the daylights out of us. I have scars from broken bones that were not properly set. My appendix ruptured because I was too scared to mention the pain. Today, my parents are still together—55 years of making each other miserable. I'd like to tell parents everywhere—don't stay with a mate you despise for religious reasons or because splitting up would be hard on you financially. Your children would rather be poor and loved.

*(Q) Is it right to stay together, even for good reasons, when there is no love between a couple?*

**3.** There should be one question for women who are in unhappy marriages: Are you better off WITH him or WITHOUT him? No woman should stay with a man who is involved with drugs or who is physically violent. She could end up dead. On the other hand, a woman who has no marketable skills and perhaps four children under 10 should not rush to divorce court just because her husband doesn't pay enough attention to her.

*(Q) Is financial independence necessary for divorce?*

- **horrendous :** terrible; dreadful
- **nasty :** very unpleasant
- **take (sth) out on (sb) :** cause (sb else) to suffer for (sb's) own misfortune or dissatisfaction
- **beat the daylight out of :** hit severely
- **scar :** mark on the skin after a wound or an injury has healed
- **rupture :** break
- **marketable skills :** money-making abilities

**4.** I don't regret my parents' divorce. It is their marriage that I regret. My parents split when I was 27. I only wish they had done it sooner. Children are NOT victims of divorce; they are victims of unhappy relationships.

*(Q) Whose interests must be considered first when thinking about a divorce, those of the couple or of their children?*

**5.** Why so many divorces? I believe it is the yuppie mentality at work—the concept that there is something newer and better just around the corner. We trade in people like cars these days. Most marriages today fall apart because the wife has to compete with the women in the workplace. My husband always left the house in the morning looking and smelling better than he ever did at home. Of course, the inevitable↓ happened. Am I glad I'm divorced? Yes. Life with a cheater↓ is hell.

*(Q) Why are people in a hurry to divorce? What accelerates divorce rates? Who is to blame? Is society partly at fault?*

**6.** I'm sorry I divorced. The worst pain of my life was seeing a picture of my children with their dad's other family. I suddenly realized that my kids had a whole other life, and I wasn't part of it. I was heartsick.↓

*(Q) Why do you think people often regret their divorce later on?*

**7.** After 25 years of marriage, my husband and I are getting a divorce. This decision was not made lightly. We both gave it plenty of thought.

We have raised two lovely daughters of whom we are very proud, and, while this is a sad time for them, they realized long ago that ours was not the perfect marriage.

We have spent hours with marriage counselors and lived in separate dwellings on more than one occasion. It hasn't all been bad or we wouldn't have stayed together for a quarter century. In fact, we have enjoyed many good times, which will be locked in our hearts forever. It's just time to move on.↓

Unfortunately, our extended family↓ seems to think

- **inevitable :** impossible to avoid or prevent; certain to happen
- **cheater :** (sb) who is sexually unfaithful
- **heartsick :** extremely disappointed; very unhappy
- **move on :** begin something new
- **extended family :** family other than just a married couple and their children

divorces have to be all the ugly things they've heard them to be, and they are already saying their "good-byes"—as if the funeral⁺ were tomorrow!

Through all of this, my husband and I have remained friends, and we intend to stay that way if we can. We are still sleeping in the same bed, and we will until our house is sold.

I want people to know that if the separating parties can make the best of it, everybody else should keep from interfering. It's hard enough being treated like outcasts⁺ by the family even before the papers are signed.

*(Q) Who do you think are more eccentric, those who get divorced or who stay married for a long time?*

**8.** Marriage is a contract where both parties pledge⁺ themselves "till death do us part." In many ceremonies, the attending guests act as witnesses and are given a charge to do all they can to support the marriage. Family and friends are to call the couple into accountability⁺ to keep the holy vows they have taken. The breakup of a marriage is not just a matter for the couple; it's a serious situation for family and friends and the whole community. For society to continue to function, we need to remind one another of our obligations, and encourage and support one another as much as we can. Friends and family must have the courage to speak up for the best interests of all involved.

*(Q) Do you think family and friends should have a duty to try to prevent an unhappy couple from separating?*

**9.** A couple divorcing after many years of marriage should know each other very well. And who, other than themselves, can know the amount of pain and misery they may have endured in their marriage? While divorce is never a picnic, it's preferable to living out one's years in a loveless marriage, or even worse, having it end in a homicide⁺ or suicide.

*(Q) Should people be ashamed if they are divorced? How should society treat them?*



- **funeral :** the ceremonies for a dead person before burial or cremation
- **outcast :** (sb) who is rejected by society
- **pledge :** vow; offer or guarantee by a solemn binding promise
- **accountability :** responsibility
- **homicide :** killing a human

# PART 2

# 25 Topical Dialogues

# Issue 26 Married to a Mama's Boy

M : I had to break up with my girl friend yesterday. I feel miserable.

F : What! How long have you been dating? Five years?

M : Closer to six, actually. She was everything I ever hoped for in a woman.

F : Then why did you break it off? Didn't she want a permanent commitment?

M : No, it was nothing like that. She feels as bad about it as I do.

F : What happened?

M : Well, the long and the short of it is that she just never pleased my mother. That was why we waited so long to get married, hoping time would bring mom around to the idea.

- **the long and the short of it :** the essential point or end result
- **bring (sb) around to the idea :** convince (sb)

F : Let me get this straight.* You dated the woman of your dreams for six years, you were both happy with each other and looking forward to spending your lives together, and you ended it because your mother was dissatisfied?

M : That's right.

F : How could you do that? Your mother's already married, it's not her life! How can she interfere with your future?

M : No, my mother and I are very close. She means everything to me. It's my duty to obey her in all things.

F : No, it's your duty to respect her and to consider her advice. But you're an adult. Ultimately, you have to make your own decisions about your own life. She can't do that for you.

M : You don't understand. She's all alone and absolutely depends on me. When I get married, I can't leave home and live on my own, I'll have to stay and take care of her. And of course, my wife will have to move in too. So it's necessary that they be able to get along.

F : Why don't you just take your mother on your honeymoon with you, then? Or, even better, why don't you just marry your mother!

M : You seem more upset about this than I am!

F : I get very upset whenever anyone, especially someone I like, lets someone run his life for him. When you were 10, you needed to be a good little boy and do whatever your mother asked. But you're not 10, anymore! You

* let me get this straight : I want to see if I understand this completely

need to stand on your own two feet. Where's your backbone?

M : You know I work very hard. On the job I have a lot of responsibility and a reputation for getting things done.

F : That's right. At work, you're one of the toughest people there. You're tenacious and tireless on behalf of your company's interests. You never take no for an answer. That's how you got where you are so quickly. But we're not talking about work! We're talking about your life! If you showed half the independence towards your mother that you show towards your boss, you wouldn't have this problem.

M : But I can't just abandon her in her old age.

F : No one is suggesting that you abandon her. But you're not in her womb anymore. You need to breathe on your own, you need to go your own way. Sooner or later, she'll be gone. Then where will you be? Too old to get married and too young to be alone! Not a very pleasant future, if you ask me.

M : When that happens, I'll try to patch up my relationship with my old girlfriend.

F : Why should she wait for you? She's already waited six years. Don't you think she has a right to a future, with or without you?

M : Or I'll find someone else, I guess. Or maybe I'll find

---

- **stand on your own two feet :** be independent
- **backbone :** courage; fortitude
- **toughest :** strongest; most persistent
- **tenacious :** unwilling to give in
- **patch up :** settle or smooth over; repair

someone that meets my mother's approval, and I won't have to wait for her to die.

**F** : No, I doubt that. I don't believe anyone is perfect enough for your mother. Why should she want to share you, when she has absolute control over you?



## Questions

1. *Explain the man's point of view.*
2. *What is his friend's point?*
3. *How would you resolve this situation?*

# Issue 27 Married vs Single

**M** : Don't you ever regret being single?

**F** : There are times when I regret not having found someone to share my life with. But since I never did, I don't regret not being married.

**M** : No desire for children?

**F** : Once in a while. Like lots of other things, we sometimes wish for what we don't have. But this has never been a great problem for me. If I ever really wanted to have children, I could have. You don't have to be married, you know! No sperm ever examined a marriage certificate before entering an egg.

**M** : And, I guess, single-parent adoptions are also possible.

**F** : That's still the exception to the rule. But I never pursued this option, so I guess I never really wanted to be a parent.

**M** : Do you miss being married, at all?

**F** : One can't miss what one never had, can one?

**M** : Aren't you worried about no one to take care of you in your old age?

**F** : I've planned well for my future, thank you. But it is just as likely that it would have been me who had to take care of someone else in old age! After all, the men are usually older than their wives, and they don't live as long on average. So, statistically, the most likely result would be that when I got old I'd have to take care of some sick old man, and then he would die and I'd still be alone with no one to care for me. I'm better off this way.

**M** : So you recommend being single?

**F** : Not really. It depends on circumstance and individual preference. But I certainly think people should have more options available to them.

**M** : Options?



- **once in a while :** sometimes; occasionally
- **egg :** female sex cell of humans
- **statistics :** the science that deals with the collection, analysis, and interpretation of information in numerical form

F : Staying single. Being celibate. Having one or more lovers but without ever marrying any of them. Having as many wives or husbands as desired. Same-sex marriages. Contract marriages. Permanent relationships without any formal legal definition. One-night stands. Open marriages without sexual exclusivity. Traditional monogamous marriages. Not being worried over age or class differences in choosing one's partners.

M : But most of these arrangements don't work well!

F : None of them work well for everyone! Not even traditional marriages! But people are different and they have different needs. Any way they can meet those needs should be okay as long as everyone involved benefits. It's time for society to stop telling us how to live our own private lives!

M : You've given me too much to think about. I need to go home and talk this over with my wife.

F : I'm not making any recommendations. I just think people need to do what's right for themselves.



## Questions

*1. Why doesn't she regret being single? Why doesn't she miss being married?*

*2. What is the connection between being married and having children?*

*3. What is her recommendation?*

- **celibate :** not engaged in sexual activity
- **one-night stand :** casual, short-term sexual relationship
- **monogamy :** the having of only one spouse at a time

# Issue 28 For Men & Women

**F** : Do you agree that women are as intelligent as men?

**M** : Sure. There's the same range of intelligence, the same bell-shaped curve, that applies to men.

**F** : Are they physically as strong?

**M** : Not for the most part, no. Of course there are very small, weak males, and very large, strong women, but the average size for adults is quite different.

**F** : Is that important?

**M** : It probably depends on the circumstances. But even jobs that used to depend on physical labor have now been mostly mechanized, so women should be able to operate the machinery as easily as men. There are probably a few exceptions, but I can't think of many.

**F** : What about emotionally? Are there any differences?

**M** : There are social differences. Men are trained at an early age not to cry or openly express their feelings, while girls are encouraged to do so. But the same human emotions are contained within them, no matter which gender they are. Neither sex is "more emotional," though one may be allowed to be more "emotive."

**F** : What about the maternal instinct? Is there such a thing?

**M** : There is a parental instinct. Men can't (yet) physically bear children, but they have the same nurturing, protective, loving nature as women. Single male parents generally do about as well raising their kids as single female parents. But among traditional families, men are

- **bell-shaped curve :** graph showing a normal statistical distribution
- **contain :** include
- **emotive :** strongly expressing (one's) feelings

still usually away from their children more than women are. Increasingly, the television and computer games are edging out not only parents but even teachers as the primary care-givers for school-aged children!

**F** : Then, are you saying there is no difference between men and women?

**M** : No, not at all. There are dozens of subtle differences. Information seems to be processed differently. There are structural differences in the body. Of course, there are different hormone balances. More differences are being found all the time. But we don't really know how these little differences affect social roles. It seems like, in terms of having a job or raising a family, the differences are unimportant.

**F** : Then why do men and women behave as though they are members of distinct species?

**M** : That's a good question! I sure don't have any answer to it.



## Questions

1. *In what ways are men and women alike or similar?*
2. *How are they quite different?*
3. *Does the dialogue imply that the differences are mainly biological or social? Explain your answer.*

---

- **edge out :** beat (sb or sth) by a small margin
- **subtle :** not immediately obvious
- **species :** members of the same animal or plant group

# Issue 29 Money and Friends

**F** : You look very happy. Where are you going?

**M** : To the bank.

**F** : Did you suddenly come into a fortune?

**M** : No. But a friend who borrowed some money from me finally paid me back.

**F** : When did you make the loan?

**M** : Actually, it's been almost 10 years. I had given up on ever getting any of it back.

**F** : Ten years! That's a long time! What finally happened?

**M** : Out of the blue, my friend contacted me last week. He's had a lot of bad fortune dogging his heels, and had always felt embarrassed about not repaying me. He'd always wanted to, but couldn't. The guilt was a very heavy burden, he told me. That's why he couldn't call me until he had the money.

**F** : I can well imagine! If I ever owe somebody, even if it's only a dinner, I feel terrible until I can do something about it.

- **come into :** inherit
- **give up on :** stop hoping for (sth) to happen
- **out of the blue :** suddenly, unexpectedly
- **dog one's heels :** follow closely behind
- **embarrassed :** ashamed, uncomfortable, ill at ease

**M** : Me, too. When I loaned him the money, it was a very open-ended arrangement. Because I knew the desperate straits he was in, I never set a deadline for repayment. I just assumed he'd take care of it as soon as he could. But I never thought it would take that long!

**F** : I would have given up a long time ago and written it off as a bad debt and him as a bad friend.

**M** : Fortunately, he turned out to be a very good friend, after all. He not only paid me back the entire sum, but also a very generous "interest" payment, though that had not been part of the deal. He's also promised to return the favor, if I ever need help.

**F** : No wonder you look so happy. You've not only got your money back, but your faith in human nature as well. You're a lucky man.

**M** : Well, I've not always been so fortunate. Most of the other times I've made a friendly loan, I've been sorely disappointed. I don't know how much money I've lost that way.

**F** : Then why did you keep making those loans? Once bitten, twice shy! I know I would never have made that mistake again.

**M** : I don't know. I guess in the long run, the money just didn't matter. I'll never really miss it, in the scheme of things. Maybe over the course of a lifetime, I could have used it to buy a new car or something, but it was never a huge sum all at once.

**F** : A new car! That's a lot. Why did you keep doing it?

**M** : Well, I always felt sorry for my friends' difficulties and wanted to help them. If I didn't do all that I could for them, I would've felt unworthy.



- open-ended arrangement : having no termination date
- straits : position of difficulty, distress, or need
- write off : cancel an unpaid debt, or a debt that cannot be collected
- bad debt : unrepayable loan
- once bitten, twice shy : cautious after being harmed (by sth)
- scheme : the way things seem to be organized

**F** : Unworthy! It seems to me that they're the ones who proved unworthy.

**M** : Yes, but maybe the rest of them will pay me back in time, too. I still have some faith in them.

**F** : You're a much better person than I. If it were me, I'd keep hounding[+] them until they relented.[+]

**M** : If you're going to act like that, why make the friendly loan in the first place?

**F** : I agree. I probably wouldn't, except in really unusual circumstances.

**M** : I just can't live like that. If the time came when I ever need help myself, I could never ask for it unless I'd tried to help others when they needed some support. That's what's friends are for, right?



## Questions

1. *What do you think about the friend who paid the money back?*
2. *Why would the man feel unworthy if he didn't help his friends?*
3. *What does "once bitten, twice shy" mean?*

---

→ **hound :** persecute; harass
→ **relent :** finally agree to (sth) after refusing

# Issue 30 Getting Rich Quick

**M :** Someone I met last week just told me about a get-rich scheme that he's privy to. He doesn't have enough money himself to finance his participation, so he wants me to join him in the venture. What do you think?

**F :** Off hand, I think it would be the stupidest decision you ever made.

**M :** Why?

**F :** First off, you don't know this man very well. How can you trust him?

**M :** We do business all the time with perfect strangers, every time we buy stock. The people who put money into Microsoft in the beginning are all multi-millionaires now.

**F :** Even then, they were affluent people who had at their disposal some capital that they could afford to lose. They probably put money into many other enterprises as well, but lost money. That's what "speculation" means: risking that which is unnecessary in hopes for a big payoff.

**M :** Then what's the difference between the stock market and gambling at the race track?

**F :** At least one of the horses is bound to win! Some bettor will always win there, which is not always true for stocks and bonds.

**M :** But, on average, investors always do well over time.



---

- **privy to :** sharing knowledge of (sth) private or secret
- **off hand :** casually; at first glance; without knowing much or thinking deeply (about the matter)
- **first off :** in the first place
- **affluent :** having a relative abundance of money or material goods; wealthy
- **at (one's) disposal :** available for (one's) use
- **capital :** wealth in the form of money or property that has accumulated and, often, is used to create more wealth; money which is indirectly earned as through interest, dividends, rent, etc.
- **enterprise :** a business
- **bound :** certain

F : No. The market tends to strengthen over time, but not necessarily individual investors. Maybe the market is going up, but the companies I've invested in may all be going bankrupt.

M : But what about Microsoft?

F : Bettors at the race track can choose between horses that are likely to win and those that aren't. Each individual "sure thing" doesn't pay off very well, because there is little risk involved, but in the aggregate is likely to make some money. The long shots almost always lose, but every once in a while one of them comes in and makes a huge profit for his backers. But the ones who constantly bet on the long shots are guaranteed suckers who will lose their shirts day in and day out.

M : Then what do you think I should do? If the guy I know is right and I turn down this opportunity, and then someone else takes him up on it and makes a fortune, I'd feel pretty stupid.

F : Don't you think you'll feel awfully bad after you throw away all your hard-earned money?

M : Well, yes, of course. That's why I don't know what to do.

F : OK. First, take a good hard look at your own financial situation and determine just how much you can afford to lose if worse comes to worse. Don't go beyond that figure, no matter what happens.

M : All right, I think that's smart. Then what?

F : Don't rush into anything until you check out the situation. Look into this man's background, find out if he has a track record. Maybe he's a crook who has

---

- **in the aggregate :** as a whole
- **long shot :** (sth) with small chance of success
- **backer :** one who supports or aids a cause or activity
- **sucker :** one who is easily fooled
- **lose (one's) shirt :** lose a lot of money
- **day in and day out :** every day for a long time
- **track record :** past achievements and failures

defrauded many in the past. If so, clearly, don't get involved.

**M** : What if he has no track record at all? Isn't that like a credit agency—it doesn't know if a prospective borrower is a bad risk unless he's already failed to pay his debts? Or like someone who can't get a job without experience, but can't get any experience without a job?

**F** : Yes, it is the same. I never said that any decision is risk-free, we always have to take some chance, but you have to reduce the risk as far as possible.

**M** : So, what if the man checks out?

**F** : Find out as much as you can about the opportunity. Don't be afraid to seek professional advice. The more thoroughly you do your homework, the better off you're likely to be.

**M** : Everything you've said makes sense. Do you have any more words of wisdom for me?

**F** : Most importantly of all, don't be blinded by greed. Keep your eyes wide open, and take your time before you make up your mind.



## Questions

1. *Why would making this investment be "the stupidest decision you ever made"?*
2. *How can one reduce one's risk in making an investment?*
3. *What is the best advice of all?*

- **defraud :** take (sth) from (sb) by dishonest methods; swindle
- **prospective :** potential; probable
- **checks out :** in shown to be reliable

# Issue 31 Lessons for Life

**M** : Let me tell you what you should do.

**F** : How can you possibly know that? It seems to me that I'm the only one who can make that decision.

**M** : Because of my experience, expertise, and authority, I possess the final answer.

**F** : But you do not walk in my shoes or see the situation through my eyes. You may have a very sound position on the problem, in the abstract, and I'd certainly be willing to hear you out—but I'm the one who has to live with the results of my actions, not you.

**M** : You are too caught up in the process to look at the issue in an objective, dispassionate manner. That is why you need outside, expert advice.

**F** : The personal aspect of the situation is precisely the reason why external guidance is irrelevant.

**M** : No. You can't see the forest as a whole because you see only the trees in front of you. Your perspective is too narrow, and you are emotionally too close to the problem. You need a broader, more comprehensive, point of view.

- walk in (one's) shoes : be in the situation or circumstances of another, so as to feel or know what the other feels or knows
- in the abstract : in theory
- hear out : listen to all of what (sb) wants to tell
- objective : not influenced by emotion or personal feelings
- dispassionate : not influenced by strong feelings or prejudice
- perspective : view; mental outlook
- comprehensive : including much; thorough

**F** : It is not just an exercise in cold logic. My whole life and the way I live it are at stake. The consequences and benefits are all mine to bear or enjoy, no one else's. That's why I have to make up my own mind.

**M** : You feel that way now, because you are so caught up in the situation. But, later, you will come to see that I am right after all. Trust me.

**F** : Trust is a fine attitude, but it pales next to individual accomplishment. Trust is for children; foresight and determination are for everyone else.

**M** : So, what are you going to do? Entirely disregard everything I know?

**F** : No. I want to hear your best advice and weigh it against the things I know and want. I wish your wisdom to be part of my decision-making process—a very valuable part—but I reserve the final judgment for myself.



## Questions

1. *What is a difference between children and adults, according to the dialogue?*
2. *Why should expert advice be sought out?*
3. *Why might it be necessary to disregard professional opinion?*

- **at stake :** at risk
- **pale :** become less important relative to (sth) else
- **reserve :** delay; postpone; set aside

Issue 32

# How to Raise Your Child

**M** : I never thought that raising kids could be so hard!

**F** : Yes, it can. And you won't know how you've done until the process is nearly over. It might take 20 or 30 years to discover what you've done right and what you've done wrong, and it's too late, then!

**M** : Thanks. You're a big help.

**F** : Well, there are manuals that you can put to good use. A lot of them, in fact.

**M** : That's what I need, a good blueprint!

**F** : None of the roadmaps are done to scale, unfortunately. They are general guides, not specific ones. There's still plenty of room for error.

**M** : What do you suggest? I think you've done a good job as a mom.

**F** : You want a recipe? OK, here goes. You need a cup of consistent discipline, added to two cups of unconditioned love. Add a spoonful of patience and a smidgeon of an allowance. Don't skimp on the ingredients. Mix well, and be sure to serve large helpings.

- **manual :** book of instructions
- **blueprint :** carefully worked-out plan, esp. architecturally
- **room :** space; occasion; possibility
- **smidgeon :** very small but indeterminate amount
- **allowance :** some small, regular payment
- **skimp :** be stingy

M : Sounds delicious. But what does it taste like, really?

F : Every dish comes out different. That's the interesting thing about it, the lack of predictability. But one thing's for sure: good results are guaranteed.

M : What if I juggle the proportions? Is that OK?

F : Sure! The best chefs never slavishly follow a recipe, they just get the best ingredients available and play by taste.

M : So, you're telling me that there are lots of good ways to do this?

F : Absolutely! As long as you keep the basic formula intact, you can do lots of variations. If you make a mess of it one day, it's almost impossible to spoil the entire meal. Just clean up and start all over again.



## Questions

1. *Why is parenting so difficult?*
2. *In what ways are being a successful parent like being a good cook?*
3. *What is the basic formula for raising children well?*

- **juggle :** balance; change relationships among
- **proportion :** size, amount, or extent of (sth) compared with that of another
- **chef :** cook
- **slavishly :** thoughtlessly, blindly without individual variation
- **play by taste :** Adjust according to flavor
- **formula :** list of ingredients and processes used to prepare (sth)
- **intact :** not weakened, injured, or damaged

# Issue 33 Stop Berating Yourself

**M** : I'd like to chat some more, but I've gotta run.

**F** : What's the hurry?

**M** : I have a string↓ of business appointments all day. I probably won't get home until 10:00 tonight. Maybe later.

**F** : Do you do this every day?

**M** : Pretty much. Why?

**F** : That was my question to you: Why?

**M** : What do you mean?

**F** : Why do you work so hard all the time?

**M** : To make money, of course! To succeed in life! That's obvious.

**F** : You call this living?

**M** : Of course! I live in a big house. I own three apartments. I have a big car and a driver. I wear expensive suits. My wife is young and beautiful, and my children all go to the best schools. So I don't understand your question.

**F** : How much time do you spend at home? When do you ever see your family? Do you have any free time to yourself, when you can do whatever you want?

**M** : I'd like to see my family more, but I'm willing to sacrifice my time with them in order to give them the things they need. As for your other point, I thoroughly enjoy my job. If I'm on vacation, I miss it!

**F** : You're just a poor workaholic,↓ I guess. I feel sorry for you.

**M** : What's to feel sorry for? I know where you live—it's small and old. You drive a used car. You never have enough money to do the things you want.

**F** : That's not entirely true. I admit that my life lacks big-ticket↓ items like expensive vacations and such. But my house is adequate to my needs, and my car gets me to

→ **string :** several similar things or events coming one after another
→ **workaholic :** (sb) who is always working and does not have time for anything else
→ **big-ticket :** very expensive

work and back every day. And I have the freedom to nurture my soul.

**M** : Whatever that means!

**F** : It means I spend lots of time with my family. We do something together nearly every day, and we're very close to each other. And I can read or paint when I want to. Or just relax and watch TV. I'm never going to be rich in material things, but I already have a rich life.

**M** : You just don't know what you're missing!

**F** : Neither do you.



## Questions

1. *Define the two attitudes toward success.*
2. *Compare and contrast the two lifestyles.*
3. *What are the shortcomings in the lives of the two people?*

---

- **nurture :** help (sb) or (sth) grow or develop; cultivate
- **Whatever that means! :** expression of skepticism toward (sb)'s explanation
- **shortcoming :** fault or problem

Issue 34

# Part-time Job

**M** : I want to get a job.

**F** : But you're still in school. Don't you need to study?

**M** : Of course I do! Do I look like a genius?

**F** : No. You look like an ordinary student. One who needs to study hard to get good grades. Nothing wrong with that, that's most people.

**M** : But I'm bored with studying! I want to do something else for a change!

**F** : Then go out with your friends. See a movie.

**M** : But I never have enough money! If I had a job, I could do that more often. Then I could force myself to study more effectively and I wouldn't waste so much time daydreaming and reading the same sentence over and over.

**F** : You just need a little discipline, that's all.

**M** : I agree. That's why I want a part-time job. It would force me to become more disciplined.

**F** : But what would you do?

**M** : I don't know. Work in a fast-food restaurant, I suppose. The hours seem flexible enough, and I should be able to work around my class schedule.

**F** : Have you ever done that?

**M** : No. I've never had any job.

**F** : It's not as easy as it looks. It's a really hectic, busy place to work. You always have to be doing something constructive, put up with a lot of rude customers—and rude bosses, too!—and you have to smile like an idiot no matter what

---

- **genius :** person of extraordinary ability, intelligence, or creative power
- **daydream :** have a pleasant series of thoughts imagined while awake
- **flexible :** capable of or willing to change; adaptable
- **hectic :** full of intense activity, confusion, or excitement
- **constructive :** serving a useful purpose or helping to improve (sth)
- **put up with :** endure (sb) or (sth) without complaints

happens! It's a real stressful job. And you sure don't get much money for it, either!

**M** : It sounds like you've done it.

**F** : I tried it one summer. I hated it! I quit after one week.

**M** : Then what did you do?

**F** : Nothing! I just played around with my friends during the day and went home every night. I didn't have any real expenses, and my parents gave me the little bit of money I needed.

**M** : But I don't want to do that! I've done that long enough. I want to start making my own way. Then I'll be in control of my own life, and I won't have to do what someone else tells me.

**F** : Nobody at all, except your boss. And your customers! Only the rich do what they like.

**M** : Well, then, the only way I'm ever going to be rich is if I start working. I sure don't have any wealthy relatives I can inherit a fortune from.



## Questions

1. *What is the value of having a job?*
2. *What are the disadvantages of work?*
3. *Why is he interested in working in a fast-food restaurant?*

# Issue 35 Before Getting Married

**M** : My daughter is getting married next week.

**F** : Congratulations!

**M** : Thanks. She would have gotten married sooner, but her fiance wasn't ready to sign a prenup.

**F** : A what?

**M** : A prenuptial agreement. You know, a contract that spells everything out if the marriage doesn't work. Who gets what property, custody of the children. Everything.

**F** : I can understand why he didn't want to sign such a document! It seems to me like a prediction that the marriage is going to fail.

**M** : Maybe. But, statistically speaking, it might fail anyway, and at least this way they're both prepared. Just because someone has a fire insurance policy doesn't mean that there'll be a fire, but anyone without one is tempting fate.

**F** : A fire is a natural, random event. It can happen anywhere. But marriage and divorce are dependent on human decision. People enter into them of their own free will.

---

- **prenup :** prenuptial agreement
- **spell out :** explain plainly
- **work :** have the desired effect or result
- **tempt fate :** do (sth) that involves risk and may cause serious problems

**M** : Of course they do. The same way they sign an employment contract. No one wants to do work for someone else without knowing how much pay there will be and when payday is. It's the same thing. A prenup is just an understanding in advance in case things don't work out.

**F** : Two people should enter into matrimony expecting it to last for life. If they're already looking for a lifeboat even before the ship leaves port, they aren't very confident about it lasting, are they?

**M** : They're merely being prudent. After all, the TITANIC was supposed to be unsinkable, and it went down on its maiden voyage.

**F** : But if the passengers had known that in advance, they wouldn't have gone!

**M** : But they didn't know, did they? And there weren't nearly enough lifeboats. A little bit of forethought could have saved hundreds of lives.



## Questions

*1. Why does he think prenuptial agreements are a good idea?*

*2. Why does she disagree with him?*

*3. Do you think the analogy with the TITANIC is apt? Why or why not?*

- **matrimony :** act of condition of being married; marriage
- **prudent :** wise in handling practical matters; sensible; careful
- **maiden voyage :** the first journey that a ship makes
- **forethought :** thought, planning, or consideration for the future
- **apt :** exactly right for a particular situation or purpose

# Issue 36 Love or Selfishness

**M** : I don't know what to do.

**F** : Can I help?

**M** : I don't know. Probably not. This is something I have to figure out on my own, I guess.

**F** : Well, why don't you tell me about it?

**M** : I think I'm in love.

**F** : Great!

**M** : No, it's not.

**F** : Why not?

**M** : You just don't understand. I promised my wife I wouldn't marry anyone else.

**F** : Of course not! That's against the law! But I'm confused. You're married?

**M** : Not any more. Yes, in a sense.

**F** : Wait! Please make up your mind. Are you married or not?

**M** : I was. But my wife died less than a year after our wedding.

**F** : That's terrible!

**M** : I know. I can't get over her.

**F** : But that means you're not really married anymore. You're free to get married again, you know. So that's good, right?

**M** : Not so good, no.

F : Why not?

**M** : Because I promised my wife I'd never get married again. I'd feel like a liar if I got married now. But, on the other hand, I don't want to give up my new love either. That's why I don't know what to do.

F : How about if you just lived together without getting married? That way, you could have your cake and eat it too.↓ You could be happy without breaking your promise.

**M** : No, I couldn't do that. That would be a sin. It has to be marriage or abstinence.↓ Those are the only two choices.

F : Okay, then, the answer is easy. Marry her!

**M** : But what about my promise?

F : Circumstances change. You made the promise with the best of intentions. But that was a long time ago. She isn't around any more—through no fault of your own.↓ But if she isn't alive, she can't blame you for breaking your word. And surely she'd want you to be happy, wouldn't she? You owe it to yourself↓—you still have a long life ahead. Make the most of it.

**M** : You make it sound so easy. But I still don't know.



## Questions

1. *What is the woman's first suggestion for solving the problem?*
2. *Why won't it work?*
3. *What is the woman's final suggestion? Will the man take her advice?*

---

→ **have (one's) cake and eat it too :** simultaneously keep and consume (sth) enjoyably
→ **abstinence :** keeping oneself from enjoyment of (sth)
→ **through no fault of your own :** you are not responsible
→ **you owe it to yourself :** your first obligation is to your own happiness or success

# Issue 37 Lottery

**F** : I have a moral dilemma. I want your opinion.

**M** : Shoot. You know that I'm a paragon of wisdom on all moral issues.

**F** : Don't be so sarcastic. I know you have a lot of detached common sense, so I'd be interested in hearing your opinion.

**M** : But on matters of morality, no one can really make the decision except you.

**F** : Shoot,* I know that. But I'd still like your input while I'm trying to decide.

**M** : Okay, I'll do my best. But don't expect too much from me.

**F** : Fine. Here's the problem. I just won the lottery.

**M** : Wow! That's great! How is this a problem? You don't know what to buy for me?

**F** : Don't be silly! But it's actually a rather small amount. I'm not rich or anything, but it's nice to have a little extra money for the holidays, you know?

**M** : So what's the problem, then?

**F** : It's like this. A friend at work and I decided to pool our resources. Each week, we'd both buy one ticket. If I won, he'd get half, and if he won, I'd get half. That way we doubled our chances of winning.

**M** : Arrangements like that are a lot of fun, usually. Until someone wins and doesn't want to share anymore. Then it's a real problem. Is that your "moral dilemma"?

**F** : Yep. You're so smart! I knew you'd be able to give me good advice.

**M** : What are your reasons for thinking you don't owe him half of it?

**F** : Well, I know that he didn't always buy a ticket every week. I'd ask him, and he'd say that he was a little short that week or didn't have the time. But I always

- **dilemma :** situation that requires (sb) to choose between options that seem equally difficult or unfavorable
- **shoot :** go ahead
- **paragon :** perfect example
- **detached :** without emotional involvement
- **shoot* :** of course
- **pool resources :** combine money for a common purpose
- **short :** not having enough money

managed to get one every week!

**M** : Did he ever win when he did play?

**F** : No, I don't think so. But he only played one third of the time.

**M** : If he had ever won, do you think you would have been entitled to half the winnings?

**F** : Absolutely. I did my fair share of the wagering. A deal is a deal.

**M** : But there would not have been a "half" unless he actually bought a ticket that week, right?

**F** : Yes, of course. But we're not talking about sharing his winnings, he never had any, and he didn't meet his obligations.

**M** : What if he had won one time, and you had not bought a ticket that week? Do you still think you would be entitled to half?

**F** : I DID buy one every week. So your question is beside the point. He's the only one who broke the agreement!

**M** : Just answer the question. If he had won and you had not bought a ticket that week, do you think he had a moral obligation to divide his winnings with you? Even if that was the only week you missed?

**F** : No, I don't think so. I would not have honored our agreement and so I would have defaulted on my part of the bargain. I wouldn't deserve anything. That's why I don't think he deserves half.

**M** : Did you ever terminate your agreement? Did you ever tell him that he wasn't playing by the rules, so you were going to discontinue the arrangement?

**F** : No, not really. But I used to scold him whenever he didn't perform.

**M** : So the agreement is still in place, then?

**F** : Yes, I guess so. Or there wouldn't be any problem at all now, right?

---

- **wager :** bet
- **a deal is a deal:** an agreement is binding no matter what
- **beside the point :** not relevant or not important to the subject
- **default :** fail to do what is required
- **bargain :** deal
- **in place :** effective

**M** : Right. So, if he had bought a winning ticket, you'd expect half, right?

**F** : Only if I'd bought a ticket, too. And I always did! But he didn't!

**M** : I realize that. But by not buying a ticket, he cut your joint chances of winning by half. And, if you didn't buy one, you'd be cutting your chances by the same amount, right?

**F** : Yes!

**M** : And if neither had bought a ticket, there would be no chance at all of winning?

**F** : Of course!

**M** : So, the more often you both bought one ticket, the better your overall chances of winning?

**F** : Yes. This is all very obvious. I know all of this. What about my problem?

**M** : And if you were the only one to buy a lottery ticket that week, and it won, then you don't think he should get half? And if he had been the only one, you wouldn't demand your share, right?

**F** : Yes, I told you that before. That's why I am not inclined to give him any money.

**M** : Even if it ends your friendship?

**F** : Well, I guess he hasn't been that good of a friend anyway.

**M** : Then I only have one question. Did he buy a lottery ticket this week? If he didn't, then you won even though the odds were more heavily against you, making it more difficult to have the winning number. Since you don't think he's a very good friend anyway, then you wouldn't owe him anything. And he would probably be your enemy for life. But if he bought a ticket also, at least this week he lived up to his end of the bargain; even if this was the only time that he did so, the agreement would still be in effect, and so you would owe him half.

**F** : Then you think I should give him the money, even though over the life of the agreement I put much more into the system than he did?

**M** : Each week, the game started over. Some weeks, you both played, and other weeks only you played. So the odds of your winning every week changed accordingly. But the odds were not cumulative, there was no penalty that carried over. Each week you either won or lost. This week, you won. If he had a ticket too, he's entitled to half. If you don't think you can trust his word, demand to see a receipt. But, no matter what you decide, I suspect that this relationship will not continue much longer. At least one of you will be unhappy over the outcome.

## Questions

*1. How did the system double the odds of the two participants?*

*2. Why does she think that she should not share her winnings?*

*3. Why will one of them be unhappy no matter what?*

---

→ **start over :** start doing (sth) again from the beginning

→ **cumulative :** increasing or growing by steady addition or in stages

# Issue 38 A Classic Mid-life Crisis

F : Would you leave your wife just because she was more successful than you?

M : Of course not! I'd probably be too financially dependent on her to even think of leaving!

F : No, I'm being serious. Are male egos so fragile that they can't stand the idea of a woman being better than other men?

M : The world is full of insecure people, of both sexes. But I don't think this is really a gender issue, as such. It's more of an economic one—until recently, most women were not competing against men. They tended to stay home and take care of the children and the household.

F : But then why would a couple that have been married for many years break up, just because the wife brought home most of the bacon? Don't you think this shows that the man has to feel superior all the time, and can't stand being in a subordinate position?

M : Maybe. But perhaps the wife didn't spend enough time with her husband. Maybe she was working all the time, and he felt lonely and unfulfilled. Or, they may have had other problems, as well.

F : But then why would he leave her just as she was hitting the peak of her profession? Why wouldn't they have broken up long ago, or why couldn't he continue to adjust longer, if gender jealousy was not the major factor?

M : "Gender jealousy!" Whew! When I was growing up, we used to be taught that ambitious women wanted to be

- **ego :** self-confidence
- **fragile :** without physical or emotional strength; delicate
- **stand :** be able to tolerate; resist; endure
- **bring home the bacon :** provide financial support for the family
- **hitting the peak of (one's) profession :** reaching the top of (one's) field

like men and do the same sorts of things that men did. We used Freud's expression, "penis envy," to describe this situation. And now men are being accused of acting the same way, of being dissatisfied because they haven't been able to compete successfully against women. Things sure have changed!

F : So you do think that men may divorce their wives because they are too successful?

M : Not directly. I think either a husband or a wife wants to share a life with some other person and feels neglected if that person is never home because of work, or is still working all the time even when at home. A lot of middle-aged women divorce their husbands for that reason, just as he is reaching his maximum level of achievement—not because of personal jealousy but because of loneliness. Now the same phenomenon is beginning to occur in reverse—some husbands feel left out of their wives' lives and want a more fulfilling existence. It's not because they are envious of their wife's success, it's because they don't feel like they are a meaningful part of it, that's all.



## Questions

1. *What is the basis for the idea of "gender jealousy"?*
2. *What is an alternative explanation?*
3. *What do you think: Are most men too insecure in their own egos to be able to accept female domination easily? Give your reasons for your opinion.*

---

- **accused :** named as committing some unfavorable action
- **dominate :** control; have a superior position, power, or authority

# Issue 39 Search for Natural Parents

**F** : I wish I knew my parents.
**M** : What do you mean? I've met your parents.
**F** : No, they're not my real parents. I was found beside the road, wrapped in a blanket. There was no note or anything, and I was taken to an orphanage. I was only a few days old.
**M** : How long were you there?
**F** : Only a few months. Then I was taken home by my new parents—the ones you know.
**M** : I always thought they did a real good job raising you.
**F** : Me, too. I could not have chosen anyone better. They're the only parents I've ever known. And I love them very much.
**M** : When did you find out?
**F** : I never did "find out"—I always knew. It was never a secret.
**M** : So, why do you want to know your real parents? It seems to me that your adoptive ones should be enough.
**F** : Oh, it doesn't have anything to do with the ones who raised me. My relationship with them won't change. To all intents and purposes, I'm their daughter. But I have a lot of questions.
**M** : Such as?
**F** : Well, such as, for instance, "Do I have some sort of hereditary medical problem I should know about?" That would be very helpful information.
**M** : Yes, I'm sure it would. But you're a healthy woman; if something's wrong with you, it doesn't seem to have damaged you very much.
**F** : No, but I wouldn't want to pass something terrible on to my children if I could prevent it, you know?
**M** : Still, chances are remote.
**F** : Yes, but there are other questions as well. I'd like to know if I have any brothers or sisters. And I want to



- **orphanage** : public institution for the care and protection of children without parents
- **to all intents and purposes** : almost completely, or very nearly
- **remote** : slight, distant

find out why I was abandoned.
M : I'm sure it was nothing personal. Probably an economic decision more than anything else.
F : Or maybe social stigma. I don't really care why, I just want to know what the reason was. And to be able to tell them that I forgive them. And that maybe they did the right thing after all, that everything worked out all right for me, I had a wonderful upbringing. Then maybe they'll feel better about their decision, as well.
M : That's very generous of you.
F : I've thought about it a long time. I even tried to contact them. The police and the orphanage staff didn't know any more about me than I did. I even tried an appeal on television. I got a few responses, but the details just weren't right. Either the respondents were frauds, or they had some tragedy separate from my own.
M : That's too bad.
F : Yes, well, I haven't given up yet. Who knows? Maybe one day all of my questions will be answered, and I'll have two sets of great parents instead of just one.
M : Best of luck to you. But, remember, even if you don't find your real parents—or, if you do find them and they aren't what you expect—either way, there are lots of other people in your life who love you.
F : I know. I'm very lucky, I guess.



## Questions

1. *Why does she want to find her real parents? Give at least four reasons.*
2. *How old was she when she was adopted?*
3. *How does she know so much about her early circumstances?*

- **abandoned :** deserted or given up
- **stigma :** sign of shame or disgrace
- **upbringing :** the care and training received during childhood
- **fraud :** (sb) who practices deception and trickery
- **tragedy :** very sad event; disaster

# Issue 40 Corporal Punishment

**F** : Excuse me, today I have to leave earlier than usual.

**M** : Why? What's wrong?

**F** : I have an appointment with the principal of my son's school.

**M** : Oh? What's happened?

**F** : Two days ago he was paddled at school. I don't think this is right!

**M** : Was he unjustly punished?

**F** : Oh, no. I'm convinced that he was responsible for a major breach of discipline. He was involved in a fight at school.

**M** : So he did it? Then, what's the beef?

**F** : The school must maintain discipline, I'm convinced of that. Maybe even it should do a better job of that than it's currently doing. But I should have been informed of my son's actions, and I should be the one to determine how to react.

- **breach :** breakage; violation of a law or obligation
- **beef :** complaint

**M** : Too many parents these days refuse to do anything about their children's behavior, and then they complain both about the schools' attempts to take action and also about the way the younger generation behaves.

**F** : Yes, I'm sure you're right. Everything is complicated in our society. Schools are in a no-win situation, "damned if they do, damned if they don't." But I'm a responsible parent, and I refuse to let the school act so arbitrarily.

**M** : When I was a boy, if I got a spanking at school, I'd get another one at home.

**F** : That did not reduce the amount of violent juvenile delinquency, however, or do anything to make our world a safer, more peaceful place. Kids need to learn that violence in and of itself is the wrong solution to any problem, not that it is okay for the strong to use violence to enforce its own authority.

**M** : So young people should be allowed to do whatever they wish, no matter what?

**F** : No, of course not. They're not fully mature, they're not yet entirely ready to take responsibility for their own choices. Adults are both legally and morally responsible for the actions of their dependents.

**M** : Then, I don't understand what your point is. The school found your son engaged in a wrongful action and disciplined him for it.

**F** : So did I. I told him why his activity was unacceptable, and I placed a number of restrictions on him. I tried to get him to understand why what he did was wrong, and I showed him there are consequences for bad behavior. I think he's much less likely to do the same thing again. But that doesn't excuse the school for taking equally wrong actions!

**M** : How was the school in the wrong?



- **generation :** people who grow up at about the same time, often thought to have similar social and cultural attitudes
- **juvenile delinquency :** antisocial or criminal behavior by children or adolescents

**F** : The principal should have contacted me immediately and discussed the situation with me. Together, we should have reached an agreement on the most effective approach to resolving the situation.

**M** : So, you might have approved of corporal punishment if you had been consulted about it?

**F** : No, I didn't say that. Some parents don't object at all, and in some circumstances I suppose corporal punishment may be an effective measure, as long as it is conducted fairly and dispassionately. But, I personally oppose the whole idea. It's completely wrongheaded, as far as I'm concerned, to say "No one can do this" on one hand, and then consciously go ahead and do that very same thing. The only lesson from this kind of behavior is that hypocrisy is fine for the ones in power, they can do whatever they like. "Do as I say, not as I do." That's the wrong message! The real lesson should be, "Practice what you preach."

**M** : I don't disagree with your philosophy, but I don't think it's very workable. Schools are highly bureaucratic, standardized institutions. The children come from an enormous number of varied backgrounds, representing many different kinds of incomes and norms. A school must have the same policy for all, and enforce it the same way in every instance. Otherwise, only chaos would ensue.

**F** : I realize the constraints and problems school operate under. But the only way to change anything is to protest against bad rules and suggest better alternatives. That's what I'm going to do this afternoon.

**M** : Do you really think one afternoon is going to make any difference?

- **consult :** seek information or advice from (sb)
- **wrongheaded :** misguided; stubbornly wrong in judgment or opinion
- **hypocrisy :** showing or expressing feelings, beliefs, or virtues that one does not actually hold or possesses
- **chaos :** great disorder or confusion
- **ensue :** follow as a consequence or result
- **constraint :** limitation

F : Probably not. But I'm ready to spend a lot of time on this matter. The people in charge have a lot of issues to deal with, and have to try and juggle their schedules to meet all these various needs. But I'm single-minded, and don't have any other pressing concerns on my hands. Sooner or later, I expect the school authorities to cave in and come around to my way of thinking. I'm sure they will be forced to change their policies accordingly and adopt a more reasonable approach.



## Questions

1. *Is there any question of the boy's guilt?*
2. *Summarize the man's attitude.*
3. *How can the woman's beliefs be applied to situations outside this specific case?*

- **juggle :** have difficulty holding or balancing (sth)
- **cave in :** yield; surrender; give in

# Issue 41 When a Man Hits a Woman

F : I certainly don't condone violence, under any circumstances, but I don't understand why some women should automatically expect to be exempt.

M : What are you talking about? I don't think a man should ever hit a woman.

F : That's just a knee-jerk reaction! Like most other men, you've been brainwashed.

M : Say whatever you like, but I just don't think it's right.

F : Why not?

M : Well, to start off, most women are a lot smaller and weaker than most men.

F : But small men who provoke large men to violence do so at their own peril, don't you agree?

M : Men who pick on weaker men are regarded as bullies, but, sure, sometimes a really obnoxious man has it coming. Men have to defend their honor!

F : Then why isn't it all right for a man to resort to violence against an insistent, castrating woman? Isn't it possible that she has it coming, too?

M : Maybe she can't help it. The only weapon most women have is their tongues.

F : And maybe the only weapons most men have are their fists. If it's sometimes "okay" to use them against obstreperous men, why not against annoying women, too? What if the woman is bigger than the man, is it okay for him to hit her then?

M : No, she's still a woman. No matter what she does, a man has to respect her femininity.

F : What if she is actually striking him? Is it all right then?

M : It's okay for him to try to defend himself, but he can do that without hitting her.

F : Why is that "fair"? Why can the woman use physical force and the man can't?

- **condone :** forgive, overlook, or ignore
- **exempt :** freed from a duty or an obligation; excused
- **knee-jerk reaction :** responding to (sth) without thinking first
- **brainwash :** indoctrinate (sb) forcibly so that his or her beliefs are replaced with different ones; persuade (sb) by intense means, such as repeated suggestion, to adopt a belief or behave in a certain way
- **peril :** great danger
- **obnoxious :** extremely unpleasant
- **have (sth) coming :** deserve to be punished
- **castrating :** removing a man's masculinity
- **obstreperous :** unreasonably-behaving, esp. rude, noisy, or insulting
- **femininity :** quality or condition traditionally attributed to a woman

M : We still have the remnants of a code of chivalry, I suppose.

F : But chivalry disappeared with the Middle Ages. These days, women sneer at men who act with deference toward them. Just try to open the door for a liberated woman, and see where it gets you!

M : Not all women are like that. Some of them still expect special treatment from men.

F : But if she's screaming at you and calling you vile names in public, she's acting pretty "liberated," don't you think?

M : She's behaving in a very unladylike manner, yes. But that doesn't mean a man has the right to hit her.

F : Modern women don't like to be called "ladylike," don't you know that? That stereotypes them with a certain kind of behavior and attitude. They want to be as free to express themselves as men do—especially if they know they can get away with it, as most men can't.

M : Two wrongs don't make a right.

F : Absolutely! But allowing them to act in ways that men are not allowed to doesn't make them equal, it just gives them an advantage in rudeness.

M : Look! Will you knock it off? I think this conversation is getting out of hand.

F : What are going to do if I keep it up? Hit me?

M : No. But I'll walk away from you and avoid talking to you until you behave yourself and change the subject.

F : Coward!

M : If you were a man and called me that, I'd knock your block off!

F : That's my point, exactly!



## Questions

1. *Under what circumstances does he think it's okay for a man to hit a woman?*
2. *Why does she think men and women are not treated fairly?*
3. *What's wrong with being called "ladylike"?*

---

- **remnants :** remaining part of (sth)
- **chivalry :** polite and kind behavior by which men show respect to women
- **sneer :** smile or speak in an unpleasant way
- **deference :** courteous respect
- **vile :** hateful, disgusting
- **knock it off :** stop; quit; cease
- **out of hand :** out of control
- **behave yourself :** act in a way that most people think is good or correct
- **coward :** (sb) who lacks courage
- **knock (one's) block off :** hit (one) hard in the head or face

# Issue 42 Pro-life vs Pro-choice

M : I don't see how we're ever going to be able to sort out the mess over abortion.

F : Why? What do you mean?

M : I mean that advocates on both sides of the argument seem to have unassailable moral grounds for the position they take, and I don't see how any acceptable compromise is even vaguely possible.

F : What do you see as being their strongest arguments, on either side?

M : Okay, let me start with the pro-lifers.

F : Fine. What's their point?

M : It's simple, really. That killing humans before they're born is just as much an act of homicide as it would be to kill them after they're born.

F : In essence, the other side is in agreement, don't you think? But they disagree on the point at which "humanity" is defined.

M : Exactly! The opponents insist that conception is the beginning of life. Before that point, there is no life, and nothing changes afterwards. So they cannot imagine any logical alternative to that position; hence, any abortion equates with the murder of a human being.



- **sort out :** put in order
- **mess :** confusing or troublesome situation
- **unassailable :** not able to be criticized, attacked, or made weaker
- **vaguely :** slightly
- **equate :** make or consider (sth) the same or equivalent

**F** : But the pro-choice advocates↓ don't buy the idea of conception↓ as equivalent to being human. An embryo, a fetus, are potentially human, but not yet so, not until they develop sufficiently to exist on their own outside the womb.↓

**M** : Yes, basically. The problem with that argument is that the moment of becoming human is not very clearly defined, so it is hard to operationalize it in any consistent sense legally. The idea of human existence from conception onwards is pretty straightforward, a woman is either pregnant or she isn't. There is no gray area.↓

**F** : So the pro-life position is the preferable one, on logical grounds.

**M** : In a binary sense:↓ either something exists or it does not. Although I don't think most pro-lifers attack abortion on purely logical grounds; it's primarily a moral, emotional response, much like the demands for an end to slavery in the nineteenth century: the notion that such a gross↓ evil should not be allowed to exist.

**F** : Okay, then, what about the pro-choice position? Do they have a leg to stand on?↓

**M** : Yes, they certainly do! If we believe that human beings should essentially be in control of their own bodies, then nobody has the right to insist that a woman remain pregnant. In the same way that we should not subject↓ other human beings to slavery, because that condition deprives them of the right to make their own choices.

**F** : So women have the right to make a selfish decision, even at the expense of↓ the baby—doesn't the child have the right to live?

---

- **advocate :** (sb) who speaks in favor of (sth); support
- **conception :** the process by which a female animal becomes pregnant, or the time when this happens
- **womb :** the part of a female's body housing a baby before birth
- **gray area :** not black or white; indeterminate, having qualities of both
- **binary sense :** having only two values, ie "yes" or "no"
- **gross :** very easy to see; obvious
- **have a leg to stand on :** have a way of proving that (sb) is right about (sth)
- **subject :** cause (sb) to undergo or experience (sth)
- **at the expense of :** at the sacrifice of; to the harm or detriment of

**M** : The "potential child," they would say. But their decision may not be entirely selfish. Many women are torn by economic and social factors, and don't want to raise their beloved children in a hostile environment. They want to wait until they themselves are more mature, have a more financially sound household, and, in many cases, have a reliable husband to share the burden. They think anything less than that would be unfair to their children!

**F** : That seems rather twisted to me.

**M** : Yes, both sides have real dilemmas if their ideas are completely adopted. Forcing a woman to have an unwanted child seems to violate the rights of both mother and child, but depriving an innocent child, who never asked to be born in the first place, of the right to live, also seems ultimately unjust and inhuman.

**F** : But the woman should have avoided becoming pregnant! She has some responsibility in the matter!

**M** : Most of the time. But it's often an impulsive act on her part. Probably alcohol is often a factor, making rational decision hard to come by.

**F** : But we don't excuse drunken drivers if they kill someone, because their normal judgment was impaired! In fact, that is why we hold them accountable!

**M** : Yes. But no method of contraception is entirely effective. A woman may have taken every conceivable step to prevent conception and still become pregnant. Not to mention cases of rape or incest, where the woman has been victimized, and giving birth to the resultant child would even further victimize her.

**F** : But don't you think fathers also have rights? Why should the baby be aborted against their will, since they have

- **torn :** badly affected
- **twisted :** strange (in an unpleasant way)
- **accountable :** expected or required to take responsibility
- **contraception :** prevention of pregnancy by drug, technique, or device; birth control
- **conceivable :** imaginable
- **incest :** sexual activity between people who are closely related, such as a parent and child or a brother and sister
- **resultant :** happening or following as a result or effect

provided half the chromosomes and will continue to share the responsibility for raising it?

**M** : Ah, that's another complicating factor. But men don't actually have to go through the physical difficulty of bearing the child, and they don't risk their own health in the process. Giving birth is painful and potentially fatal for the mother—another reason why some women don't want to stay pregnant.

**F** : Well, okay, I guess I see the problem more clearly now. Do you have any good solution?

**M** : No, not unless both sides are willing to make some key concessions to the worldview of the other. Right now, they are locked in ideological battle, with neither side willing to yield an inch, since neither is ready to recognize that the other has a valid moral point.



## Questions

1. *What is the strongest pro-life argument? What is a possible effective counter-argument against that point?*
2. *What is the strongest pro-choice argument? What is the main flaw in that argument?*
3. *When does a "human" begin its existence?*

---

- **concession :** yielding, giving in
- **worldview :** the way that (sb) sees and understands morality, esp. in relation to their religious, political or cultural beliefs and ideas
- **valid :** true; sound; just; well-founded
- **counter :** contrary; opposing

# Issue 43 Adoption

F : People who are so concerned with stopping women from having children should be more concerned with taking care of the ones we already have.

M : The ones we have?

F : You know, collectively. That the whole world has.

M : You mean society should spend more money on things like immunization and children's health screening.

F : No. Those are good ideas, to be sure, but it's not what I intended.

M : Then, what do you mean?

F : I mean we have an enormous problem with adoptions.

M : Oh. Yes, I agree. Governments are making it much more difficult for prospective parents to be able to adopt.

F : I know that the governments mostly mean well, they're trying to protect the children from abuse.

M : That's right. But for the most part adopted children are not abused; they are often treated with more loving care than natural children.

F : Statistically, I'm sure you're right. It's probably because the people who adopt them have given up on having children of their own, so this is the only parental option available to them.

M : Not all adoptive parents are childless, you know. A great many of them have children but can't stand to realize that so many other kids need good homes.

F : You make them sound like stray dogs or cats!

M : They have a lot in common, though. Strays and orphans feel lonely and unwanted, through no fault of their own.

- collectively : together, as a group
- immune : protected against a disease, as by an injection
- prospective : possible, likely, or expected; potential; probable
- stray : lost or homeless
- unwanted : unloved

Maybe their real parents have died, or maybe they were just too young or too poor to take care of them properly. But either way, the kids suffer from neglect.

F : Even if they are being properly fed and clothed—which is not always the case, believe you me—even then, they are deprived of the love of a family.

M : Why do you suppose they are treated that way?

F : Lots of reasons, I suppose. The difficulty in general of raising kids. Add to this the notion that the orphans are not blood relatives, and the sense of obligation diminishes.

M : Some people don't even want foreign couples, or people from different ethnic groups or religions, to be able to look after "their" orphans.

F : That's particularly tragic when "their" orphans are not being looked after well, and yet there are probably millions of people around the world who would love to be given the chance to take care of them.

M : I've noticed that the worst places for that sort of attitude are often the same ones that most strongly discourage their own people from adopting them as well.

F : They care too much about ancestry and not nearly enough about the needs of little children.

M : The older kids have it the worst, though. Babies have an excellent chance of getting adopted. They're too young to realize their position, and I suppose some of them never find out that their own parents aren't their "real" ones.

F : It's true. The older they get, the worse their odds become. Few people want to take on some child whose personality traits are already formed. And, of course, as their opportunity diminishes, their sense of being misfits grows. They suffer more and more as time goes on.

M : It's particularly sad in cases where some child is almost adopted many times, but something always gets in the



- **believe you me :** definitely
- **ancestry :** line of descent
- **misfits :** people who cannot adjust to their situation in life or are seen as too different from other people

way. The prospective parents change their minds, or they decide to adopt someone else, or the court or the government disallow them.

**F** : Yes. I can't imagine what it is like to suffer that kind of frustration, especially if you're an adolescent. Being a teenager with loving parents is hard enough in terms of figuring out your identity and your place in the world—those natural feelings of teenage angst must be almost unbearable to an orphan.

**M** : What can be done about it, do you suppose?

**F** : Churches and governments and welfare agencies of all kinds should start public service campaigns to promote the benefits of adoption, not only for the kids but for the adoptive parents as well.

**M** : Speaking of benefits, maybe some additional tax breaks or other kinds of subsidies should be provided to make raising them less difficult,

**F** : Right. We should all be looking for ways to make adoption easier, not ever more difficult.



## Questions

1. *Why don't more people adopt? Can you think of any reasons not mentioned in the text?*
2. *How can they be encouraged to adopt?*
3. *Why do adoptive parents often become more loving than biological parents?*

- **angst :** perpetual or persistent anxiety
- **tax break :** special reduction in taxes for a particular purpose
- **subsidy :** financial assistance, such as that granted by a government to a private business

# Issue 44 To Remember Me

**M** : Want my kidney?

**F** : No thanks, I already have two. But I'll keep it in mind.

**M** : No, I'm serious. A lot of lives could be saved if more people would just allow their viable↓ organs to be used after their deaths, when they don't need them any more.

**F** : Sounds disgusting to me.

**M** : Why should it? The technology is in place↓ for many organs, and the organizations as well. Wouldn't you rather rest in peace, knowing that even in death you have given someone the precious gift of life, than merely, selfishly, keeping your dead body intact so that it all decomposes↓ together?

**F** : It's a good thing you're not in advertising. You wouldn't persuade many people, using language and imagery like that!



- **viable :** capable of continuing to live, grow, or develop
- **in place :** in position; at the ready
- **decompose :** decay; rot

M : I'm just telling the truth. I can't think of a single rational idea why people would oppose organ-giving. If you had a pair of gloves that were perfectly good and you knew you were moving to some warm part of the world where you'd never need gloves anymore, you wouldn't be opposed to giving your gloves to some needy person, would you?

F : Of course not! But you're making a false analogy. Gloves and organs are not the same thing at all. Gloves are man-made, they're not part of you at all. But my organs are a vital part of my own life. I don't want to be mangled or dismembered if I can help it.

M : But why? Once you're dead, you have no need for a body—or body parts—any more. If the atheists are right, we're all just meat anyhow. And if the religious ones are correct and we actually have some sort of afterlife, it would be in a spiritual form—we wouldn't have a body anymore anyway. So why not help someone out with a liver or a kidney or a heart or an eye. It's exactly like the glove example, except that we're talking about saving somebody's life, not just keeping his hands warm!

F : No, I can't see it. It all sounds too much like Frankenstein's monster, for my taste.

M : I bet you'd change your tune if you or someone you loved needed a new organ in order to live and none could be found due to a lack of donors.

F : I doubt that very much. Some things just never change.

---

- **analogy :** similarity between unlike things
- **mangle :** damage or hurt (sb) seriously by twisting or crushing
- **dismember :** cut, tear, or pull off parts of a body
- **atheist :** (sb) who believes that God does not exist
- **Frankenstein's monster :** fictional monster created from corpses

**M** : And your mind is one of them?

**F** : No, but the weird unnaturalness of having someone else's heart, for example, could never be dismissed out of hand.

**M** : Sometimes it takes a good idea a long time to catch on, but usually it does, sooner or later.

**F** : Unfortunately, some really loony ideas become acceptable as well, as soon as enough people jump on the bandwagon.

**M** : But this is not a loony idea at all! It's almost a form of immortality. After I'm gone, part of me will live on in other bodies, on and on perhaps for an eternity.

**F** : Well, I only hope no one gets your brain. Nobody would deserve that!



## Questions

*1. Describe how body parts are like discarded gloves.*

*2. Why are some people opposed to donating their organs?*

*3. If you needed a new liver to survive and one could be provided to you from a dead person's body, would you reject the donation?*

---

- **out of hand :** casually
- **catch on :** understand; become popular
- **loony :** foolish or crazy
- **jump on the bandwagon :** join a party, cause, or movement that appears to be gaining popular support or becoming successful

# Issue 45 Sex Appeal

F : Do you know why the banana got married and the grape didn't?
M : OK, I give up. Why?
F : Because the grape didn't have a peel!
M : Oh! What a terrible joke that was! It's just stupid, that's all.
F : Don't you like puns?
M : No, I think they're the lowest form of humor.
F : Even lower than slapstick?
M : Actually, I don't see much difference between them. They're both just examples of childish nonsense.
F : What's wrong with being a kid?
M : Nothing is wrong with being one, if you're ten. But to be an adult, you have to grow up sometime. You can't just act like a juvenile all through your life.
F : What a humorless grouch you are!
M : I'm not humorless at all. My wife thinks I'm a lot of fun. I just prefer humor that has some sense behind it, that's all. I like satire a lot, for example.
F : Well, your wife must have a great sense of humor—after all, she married you.
M : Stop trying to get my goat! I'm in too good of a mood to let you spoil my day.
F : Why? What's today?
M : It's my wedding anniversary. I've had 10 years of happy marriage to the same wonderful woman.
F : Mmmmmm. Ten out of 20, not bad. That's batting .500!
M : For your information, it's 10 out of 10! Stop goofing off.
F : OK, I'm sorry. I guess I feel a little perky myself today.
M : Why? What happened?
F : I think I'm in love! I met the most wonderful man last week. He's been calling me half a dozen times a day, every day. My head is swimming!

---

- **puns :** humorous use of words or phrases to emphasize or suggest its different meanings or applications, or words that are alike in sound but different in meaning
- **slapstick :** comedy characterized by silly, noisy, and physically violent action
- **grouch :** person who habitually complains or grumbles
- **get (one's) goat :** anger, annoy, or frustrate (sb)
- **batting .500 :** being successful half the time
- **goof off :** waste time; be silly
- **perky :** cheerful, lively
- **swim :** be dizzy or giddy; seem to whirl

M : Well, be careful. Passion isn't everything, you know. It's one thing to love someone, but do you also like him?

F : What's the difference?

M : Do you want to spend boring times, sick times, angry and frustrating times, with this person? It's a lot easier to get through bad times with people you like than with anyone else. But to love someone requires constant excitement. Without the spark,* the explosion just can't sustain itself. Pretty soon, other emotions, like disgust and hatred, take the place of love. Or the sexual attraction continues strongly, but it feeds on* violent feelings of jealousy and possessiveness. It can be sheer* hell, even if it's also very heavenly.

F : I take it back,* you're not just a humorless grouch—you're also an unromantic one.

M : Say whatever you like, my wife and I have been happily married a long time. There isn't much "romance" in our lives anymore, as you call it, but we're very contented with each other, and we're still together through good times and bad. I'm looking forward to another 10 years, and then another 10 after that, for the rest of our lives.

## Questions

1. *Explain the "grape" joke.*
2. *What does "10 out of 20" imply?*
3. *Why does the man prefer "liking" someone to "loving" anybody?*

---

- **spark :** feeling of sexual attraction
- **feeds on :** is perpetuated by
- **sheer :** complete
- **take (sth) back:** admit that (sb) was wrong to say (sth)

# Issue 46 Is Money a Proper Gift?

**M** : I'm stuck on* a problem.
**F** : Can I help you with it?
**M** : Maybe you can give me some advice. I'm trying to decide on a birthday present for a friend.
**F** : Male or female?
**M** : Female.
**F** : How close are you?
**M** : We're just friends, it's not a romantic relationship. But we spend a lot of time together, and I can't just ignore her birthday.
**F** : So I guess something like jewelry or perfume would send her the wrong signal.
**M** : Right. And I can't give her lingerie, either.
**F** : How about clothes? Do you know her size?
**M** : I don't think she likes my taste in clothes, so she probably wouldn't wear them if I got them for her. And I don't know what she needs.
**F** : How about a good book?
**M** : No, she's not much of a reader.
**F** : A CD?
**M** : That's a good idea. But she likes classical music, and I don't know anything about it. I wouldn't know where to begin.
**F** : Take her out to a concert or a movie and a dinner.
**M** : We do that pretty often anyway. It wouldn't seem anything special.
**F** : Flowers? Candy?
**M** : No, those don't seem right.
**F**: Well, what does she like to do, then? Does she have any hobbies?
**M** : She likes to eat.
**F**: Then get her food!

* stuck on : fixated; unable to move from

M : That doesn't seem like much of a present. "Here, have a pizza for your birthday!"

F : That's a great idea!

M : It is?

F : Sure. Do something special with the pizza. Order one just before you meet her so it doesn't get cold. And gift wrap the box so she won't know what it is before she opens it. She'll remember your gift for a long time to come! She'll tell all her friends about it.

M : I don't know, it sounds sort of silly to me.

F : Trust me! She'll love it!

M : Maybe I should just give her money or a gift certificate or something. Then she can get whatever she wants.

F : But that's too impersonal.↓ It's more like a business transaction than a show of affection. Anybody can give her money, but only a real friend would take the time and care to give a really special gift.

M : But it's so hard!

F : I know, but the harder it is, the more she'll appreciate it.



## Questions

*1. Why can't he give her lingerie?*

*2. Can you guess why candy or flowers would be inappropriate?*

*3. What's wrong with giving her money?*

→ **impersonal :** lacking human emotion or warmth

# Issue 47 Every Man for Himself?

**M** : Unselfish co-operation is an amazing human attribute, don't you think?

**F** : As well as being rare.

**M** : It's not as unusual as you make out. Most people are more than willing to help out for the common good, even if they don't directly get anything out of it themselves.

**F** : That's what the hustlers want us to believe, at any rate. But behind every unselfish act is a manipulator who benefits directly.

**M** : That's a little harsh, don't you think?

**F** : Harshness does not invalidate the truth, however. The billionaires who give vast sums to charity do it for tax benefits and good public relations. It validates their status as "superior human beings," the same way that the old kings would dispense alms to the public. The more money you can afford to give away, why, clearly the more you have.

**M** : But what about the poor people who give away so much to help others? They don't benefit.

**F** : That's true, perhaps, but maybe the reason they're so poor is that they behave so foolishly. They don't give in a manner that helps themselves because they don't know any better.

**M** : You can't have it both ways. Even if it's true that a lot of self-serving people only want the appearance of being generous, you can't dismiss the genuinely kind ones as being merely stupid. The fact is that they are trying to help their fellow sufferers, even at great cost to themselves.

**F** : But that is the very attitude that is so easily taken advantage of by the con men of this world. That's why there are so many phony charities and help-the-poor scams, run by greedy extorters.



- **attribute :** quality or characteristic belonging to (sb) or (sth); distinctive feature
- **make out :** express; understand
- **help out :** aid or assist (sb)
- **hustlers :** those who deceive to gain money; con men
- **invalidate :** discredit; show that (sth) is incorrect
- **alms :** money, food, or other donations given to the needy
- **scam :** dishonest business scheme; swindle
- **extort :** obtain (sth) from another person by threats or force

M : No, I accept your point. I agree that there are a lot of bad people in the world. But, don't you see? You're trying to say they succeed in taking advantage of other people's generosity—there wouldn't be any generosity to take advantage of if everyone were like them!

F : Oh! I see what you mean. I guess you're right, logically. But that doesn't alter my original contention. I still say that there are no unselfish acts.

M : If I give all my money to the poor—or, more wisely perhaps, give the poor everything I don't need directly—or, if I give them anything at all, in fact, isn't that evidence of my unselfish generosity?

F : By no means. If you aren't interested in the tax break, or if you give anonymously so there's no public relations angle to it, I still say that you get something out of the transaction. Maybe giving relieves your sense of guilt. Maybe the reward you get is the feeling of generosity, so all you're really doing is feeding your ego-gratification. But you wouldn't do it unless you got some benefit from it. We're not by nature altruistic animals and, in fact, if we were, we couldn't survive as a species. "Every man for himself," that's the motto that made us what we are today: masters of the world!

## Questions

1. *What are the obvious benefits of philanthropy?*
2. *What are the more subtle aspects of giving to charity?*
3. *Can you think of any truly unselfish acts? Share your thoughts with the class.*

- **alter :** make (sth) different; change
- **contention :** statement put forward in an argument
- **anonymous :** nameless or unnamed
- **angle :** perspective
- **transaction :** business arrangement
- **ego-gratification :** doing (sth) that gives oneself personal satisfaction
- **altruism :** concern for the welfare of others
- **altruistic :** selflessly benevolent
- **philanthropy :** unselfish concern for human beings, esp. as shown by voluntary service or donations

# Issue 48 Childless Couple

**F** : Did you know that my sister is coming back today?

**M** : From Australia, you mean?

**F** : Of course.

**M** : How does she get to take all these trips? Her husband makes less money than I do. And yet they have a nicer home and a newer car and more fun than we do!

**F** : And they certainly don't manage their finances any better than you. It's as though they don't have any responsibility. Whatever they want, they just get.

**M** : But of course, that's the answer!

**F** : What is?

**M** : That they don't have any responsibility.

**F** : I didn't mean they were irresponsible.

**M** : No, of course not. But they don't have any ongoing responsibility. They don't have any kids!

**F** : Well, I knew that, of course.

**M** : Yes, but have you stopped to think how much money we have to spend on our kids all the time?

**F** : Clothes, books, lessons, food, medical and dental bills, entertainment....

**M** : Not to mention things like insurance, babysitting, furniture.

**F** : Bus fare. Candy. It really starts to add up after a while. By the time they finally grow up and leave home, I'll bet we will have spent over a quarter million dollars on them.

**M** : And the expense won't just stop there. Weddings, grandkids, emergencies. The list is endless.

**F** : Wow, I never really thought about this before. It just seemed like having children was the natural thing to do.

**M** : It still seems that way. I wouldn't trade our kids for all the money in the world.

**F** : Me neither. Sometimes they're a problem, and it's certainly hard keeping up with the cost week in and week out, but it's all worth it.

**M**: And of course, when we're old they'll be able to help us out. But that's not even the point.

**F** : No, the whole point of having children is to create a family. The connections between family members are more valuable than the economic considerations.



---

→ **not to mention :** in addition to

→ **week in and week out :** all the time without pause

**M** : On the other hand, your sister seems to be very happy with her husband, even though they don't have any children.

**F** : Yes, they're very happy. Sometimes I envy them, because they have the opportunity to spend a lot of time alone together. They communicate with each other extremely well, sometimes I think better than we do.

**M** : Well, between work and our kids, we don't have much time or energy left just for ourselves.

**F** : I know. Sad isn't it? That was why we got married in the first place, to be together.

**M** : I'll try to spend more time with you.

**F** : I know you mean well, but even if we had more opportunity, we'd still have to include the children. It's not the same.

**M** : I know. It isn't very romantic any more, is it?

**F** : No. But life is more than just romance, isn't it?

**M** : I guess so. Do you know why your sister never had kids? Is there some sort of medical problem?

**F** : No. They just decided they didn't want any. They agreed on that even before they were married.

**M** : But why?

**F** : They thought that kids would get in the way of their being happy together. Without children, they have the money and freedom to pursue their interests the way they want to. They can go anywhere they want, do anything, any time they please.



## Questions

1. *What are the advantages of having children? Can you think of any not mentioned in the text?*
2. *What are the disadvantages of having children?*
3. *What are the advantages of not having any?*

# Issue 49 Gender Favoritism

**M** : Did you meet your friend?

**F** : Yes, we had a lovely dinner. But she was so depressed.

**M** : Depressed? Why? Didn't she just have a baby?

**F** : Yes, but she's sorry it wasn't a boy.

**M** : What difference does that make?

**F** : It makes a lot of difference! She feels like she's a failure. Her husband really wanted a son to carry on the family name. He doesn't have any brothers, you know.

**M** : Well, it's his fault, you know?

**F** : What do you mean, his fault?

**M** : It's always the male's chromosomes that determine the children's gender.

**F** : Oh. I knew that. But it isn't his fault. He doesn't have any control over that.

**M** : I know. But it isn't her fault either. She shouldn't feel guilty or depressed about it.

**F** : That's what I told her, too. But I'm not sure she took my advice to heart.

**M** : Besides, I think little girls are great! I'm sure they're a lot easier to raise than boys, and they're so sweet!

**F** : You never had daughters, did you?

**M** : No, you're right. But am I wrong?

**F** : Girls are easy until they're teenagers, but then they're much harder than boys. You have to worry about them all the time.

**M** : They should all be treated the same, I think. Not exactly the same—not all boys or all girls are exactly alike and each needs a different kind of treatment—but their gender shouldn't matter.

**F** : The voice of experience!

**M** : Don't make fun of me just because I never had daughters. I think it's just common sense.

**F** : It's a good thing you don't have daughters, I think. They need a strong father to guide them, or they'll just take advantage of their weak dad. You'd let them do anything, I suppose!

→ **chromosomes :** genetic units that determine offspring's characteristics
→ **the voice of experience :** expert

**M** : No, but I'd give them the same guidelines that I give my sons.

**F** : And what would these be?

**M** : Be careful about your actions. Think of the consequences of what you do, and try not to hurt yourself or anybody else. What's wrong with that advice?

**F** : It's good advice. But kids need more than just advice. Children—and especially girls—need someone to think on their behalf. They haven't had much practice in making good decisions and don't know what to do. There are too many temptations and they're too naive to make good, hard choices.

**M** : It doesn't matter whether they are boys or girls, they need to start making choices at a young age, with their parents' guidance, or they will never learn how. Even though they will inevitably make some bad decisions, they have to stand on their own two feet.



## Questions

*1. Give at least two reasons why the woman should not be depressed.*

*2. According to the dialogue, are boys easier to raise than girls?*

*3. What advice would the man give, as a father? Is that advice sufficient, do you think?*

---

- **on their behalf :** for their sakes
- **naive :** lacking experience of life, knowledge or good judgment
- **inevitable :** impossible to avoid or prevent; certain to happen

Issue 50

# Divorce

**F** : Why can't two people stay together and be happy?

**M** : Some can, of course. But it's very difficult.

**F** : The people who get married are not the same people later on.

**M** : Yes, folks change. At different rates and in different directions. But that is also true for the ones who stay happily married.

**F** : What is the main reason for breaking up? Or, for that matter, for staying together?

**M** : It's useless to generalize. For most people, communication is the key. If they can continue to empathize with one another and stay open to each other's moods and attitudes, they probably both get

empathize : having the ability to identify with another's feelings or thoughts, etc., as if they were one's own something out of their marriage that they cannot get anywhere else. But even good communicators may tire of each other, and even bad ones may stick it out to the end. People are not simple!

F : When is divorce the right answer? How can one know what is best?

M : It is always a personal decision. Emotions, feelings, are a major part of the equation, but cold reason also has a role. "Am I happy?" "Would I be happier if I were not married?" "Would I be happier being married to someone else?" "Who would take care of me if I were single?" These are the kinds of questions one asks, and everyone reaches a different answer.

F : What other factors are relevant?

M : Besides individual concerns, society is extremely important. In many cultures, divorce is simply not permitted except under extreme conditions. Even then, when it is allowed, divorced people are pitied or condemned to social inferiority. Sometimes, it is easy for men to break off a union, but difficult for women to do so. And, of course, divorce rates are soaring in most modern cultures; it is not unusual at all for people to be married two or three times.

F : Do married couple need to be faithful to make the marriage last?

M : Often, it doesn't matter. Great philanderers may also be



- **tire of :** become bored with
- **equation :** problem or situation to be solved
- **cold reason :** without emotion
- **relevant :** related to; pertinent
- **soar :** rise suddenly, esp. above what is normal
- **philanderer :** playboy

excellent mates and parents. Sometimes sexual variety helps keep a marriage from becoming stale. A few couples even agree to an "open" marriage in which they do not even pretend to be monogamous but stay together quite happily. What does not seem to work very well, though, is if one partner is carrying on an affair and the other one is adamantly opposed to such behavior; when the latter finds out about the infidelity, it is almost impossible to save the marriage.

F : What do you think about unmarried people living together?

M : When the practice first became widespread a few years back, it seemed like an excellent idea. The notion was that a man and a woman would learn what the other person was like before they got married, and if they were incompatible they could separate rather easily. But the emotional attachment becomes just as strong in these cases, and it is often just as difficult to end the relationship as it is for married people to do so (though, of course, there are fewer legal entanglements, so that part is less complicated). One of the odd facts is that people who live together before getting married have even higher divorce rates than those who do not!

F : I suppose that's because they began their relationship without a real commitment, and they never allowed one to develop.

- **stale :** not interesting or exciting anymore; dull; old
- **adamant :** determined not to change
- **infidelity :** unfaithfulness, esp. to one's spouse
- **entanglements :** complications; difficulties

**M** : Yes. Or it may be that without some kind of binding obligation on each other, they both had to work harder to make the other one happy; once they get married, it is not as easy to just suddenly decide to leave, so they take each other for granted and neither of them has to devote quite as much attention to the other.



## Questions

1. *What seem to be the most ordinary components of a successful marriage?*
2. *Why do people decide to divorce?*
3. *What was the expectation about people who lived together before they got married? How did things turn out instead?*

APPENDIX

# Openers for Your Discussion!

다음은 1:1 대화나 집단토론에서 자주 쓰이는 표현
(특히 처음 시작할 때의 표현을 중심으로)을
정리해 놓은 것입니다.

| | | |
|---|---|---|
| 1) 모르는 사람에게 무엇인가를 묻기 위해접근해서 이야기를 걸때 | Pardon me<br>Sorry<br>May I interrupt for a moment? | Excuse me<br>Pardon me for interrupting, but |
| 2) 집단 토론 중에 갑자기 지적할 문제가 생겨 말을 끊고 나올때 | Sorry, but<br>May I add something?<br>May I ask a question?<br>I'd like to comment on that<br>I have a point here | I might add here<br>May I say something here?<br>Excuse me for interrupting, but<br>I'd like to say something |
| 3) 원래의 주제로 다시 돌아갈때 | Anyway<br>To return to<br>To get back to<br>Going back to<br>What were we talking about? | In anycase<br>Returning to<br>Let's get back to<br>Where was I? |
| 4) 누군가에게 무엇을 물어볼때 | I'd like to know<br>Could you tell me<br>Do you know | I'm interested in<br>Could I ask<br>Do you happen to know |
| 5) 주저하거나 망설임을 나타낼때 | Well<br>Now<br>You know | Look<br>You see<br>Listen |
| 6) 일의 순서를 나열할때 | First<br>First of all | To begin with |
| | Secondly<br>Then<br>So<br>Before you finish | Next<br>After that<br>So then |
| | At the end<br>As the last thing | Finally |

| | | |
|---|---|---|
| 7) 중요한 점을 부각 시킬때 | First of all<br>The most important thing is | The main thing is<br>Primarily |
| 8) 중요한 문제점을 지적할때 | The trouble is<br>Don't forget that<br>The awful thing is | The problem is<br>The real problem is |
| 9) 놀랄만한 사실을 이야기 할때 | Do you realize that<br>Believe it or not<br>It may sound strange (or funny), but<br>Strangely enough | Surprisingly<br>You may not believe this, but |
| 10) 새로운 사실을 이야기 할때 | Guess what!<br>Do you know what? | I've got news for you!<br>You won't believe this, but |
| 11) 일반적인 사실을 이야기 할때 | Generally<br>As a rule<br>usually<br>On the average | By and large<br>Normally<br>Typically |
| 12) 상대방에게 즐겁지 않은 사실을 이야기 하고자 할때 | Actually<br>To tell the truth<br>To be blunt | But frankly<br>To be honest |
| 13) 현실적인 이야기를 하고자 할때 | To be honest with you<br>Now be realistic | Let's face it |
| 14) 이야기의 주제를 바꿀때 | Speaking of<br>By the way<br>I just thought of something | That reminds me<br>Before I forget |
| 15) 자기의견을 이야기 할때 | I think<br>In my opinion<br>I personally think<br>I suspect<br>I'm almost positive | I imagine<br>In my estimation<br>To my mind<br>I'm pretty sure<br>I have reason to believe |
| 16) 자기확신을 이야기 할때 | I strongly believe<br>I'm convinced<br>Without a doubt | I'm positive<br>Undoubtedly |

| | | |
|---|---|---|
| 17) 개인적인 상황을 이야기 할때 | In my case<br>Personally, I'm more interested in | What I'm concerned with is<br>For my own part |
| 18) 소문 따위의 비밀스런 이야기를 하고자 할때 | I've heard<br>Just between you and me<br>I hear they say | They say<br>Rumor has it |
| 19) 어떤 제안을 하고자 할때 | Why don't you<br>If I were you, I would<br>Perhaps you could<br>Try<br>May I make a suggestion | I suggest you<br>Why not<br>How about<br>I have an idea |
| 20) 어떤 계획에 대하여 이야기 하고자 할때 | I'm planning to<br>Our plan is to<br>What we have in mind is<br>What we plan to do is | What I'm planning to do is<br>We are thinking of<br>Our scheme is |
| 21) 어떤 특정한 포인트에 대해 설명하고자 할대 | Regarding<br>As far as (something) is concerned<br>Where (something) is concerned<br>When it comes to (something)<br>In that respect<br>On that point | Concerning<br><br><br><br>As far as that goes<br>In that instance |
| 22) 특정한 상황에 대해 의견을 말할때 | In a case like this<br>In a situation like this<br>In this type of situation | In this case<br>In such a situation<br>In this instance |
| 23) 어떤 특정한 포인트를 강조할때 | That's just the point<br>But the point is<br>This raises a problem<br>But the problem with that is | But the question is<br>But the real question is<br>This raises a question |
| 24) 특정한 포인트를 추가할때 | Also<br>In addition<br>In other respect<br>Perhaps I should mention<br>Not to mention the fact that<br>Not only that, but | And another thing<br>What's more<br>I might add<br>I almost forgot<br>Plus the fact that |

| | | |
|---|---|---|
| 25) 이유를 설명할때 | The reason why<br>Owing to<br>Because<br>Since | The main reason why<br>Due to<br>Because of |
| 26) 제시된 이유에 대한 부연설명을 할때 | For this reason<br>Owing to this<br>This is why<br>That's why<br>Therefore<br>As a result<br>Thus | On account of this<br>Because of this<br>This is the reason why<br>That's the reason why<br>So<br>Consequently |
| 27) 즉각적인 대답 보다는 약간 망설임을 나타낼때 | Well, uhm<br>Let's put it this way | Well, let's see<br>I'll have to think about that |
| 28) 자기 자신의 의견(또는 의미)을 분명히 할때 | What I mean is<br>What I'm saying is<br>Don't get me wrong<br>Don't misunderstand me (on this point)<br>Let me put it another way<br>What I really said<br>You must have misunderstood me<br>Let's get this straight, I said | What I meant was<br>What I'm trying to say is<br><br><br>That's not what I said |
| 29) 무엇인가를 거절할때 | I don't care for<br>I'm not going to<br>I don't like<br>What I can't stand is<br><br>I'm not really interested in<br>I don't need<br>I don't have the time to<br>I'm perfectly satisfied with<br><br>I'd prefer | I can't stand<br>This isn't my idea of<br>I can't take<br><br><br>I'm not worried about<br>I have no use for<br>I'm not concerned with<br><br><br>I'd rather |
| 30) 질문하고 무엇인가를 제안할때 | I wonder why<br>Are you serious when you say<br>Why do you | Do you really think (or believe)<br>Isn't it true that<br>Do you mean to say |

| | | |
|---|---|---|
| | Don't you think (or say, or agree)<br>Wouldn't it be a good idea<br>I wonder if | Wouldn't it be better<br>Why don't you |
| 31) 설명을 요구할때 | Can you explain why<br>I don't understand why<br>Why is it that<br>What do you mean by<br>What do you have in mind (with) | I wonder why<br>I keep wondering why<br>Why do you think |
| 32) 어떤 계획에 대해 유보적인 입장을 취할때 | I doubt<br>I don't know if<br>Yes, but<br>Sure, but<br>I'd love to, but<br>That may be so, but<br>I don't see advantage in<br>What I'm concerned about is<br>What bothers me is<br>One drawback is | I'm afraid<br>But the problem is<br>Possibly, but<br>That's a good idea, but<br>That would be great, except<br>Yes, but the question is<br>What I'm worried about is<br>What I'm afraid of is<br>What I don't like is |
| 33) 어떤점을 고려하라고 할때 | Considering<br>Taking into account<br>If you remember<br>Allowing for the fact<br>All things considered | Seeing<br>Remembering<br>Keeping in mind<br>When you consider |
| 34) 다른 대안이 없어 굴복할때 | If there's no other way<br>If that's so<br>Well, under those circumstances | If there's no alternative |
| 35) 빈도 (Frequency)를 나타낼때 | Generally<br>As a rule<br>Ordinarily<br><br>Usually<br>Again and again<br><br>Once in a while<br>From time to time | In general<br>Mostly<br>As a general rule<br><br>Most of the time<br>Time and again<br><br>Every so often<br>Every now and then |

| | | |
|---|---|---|
| 36) 예외를 지적할때 | There are exceptions, of course<br>One should mention, of course<br>An exception to that is, of course<br>This does not include<br>Except that<br>But what about | <br><br><br>With the exception of (that)<br>One exception is<br>But think of |
| 37) 예를 들고자 할때 | For example<br>Take for example<br>For one thing<br>To illustrate my point<br>As an illustration | For instance<br>A classic example of this is<br>To give you an idea<br>Just as an example |
| 38) 요약 및 결론을 이야기 할때 | To make a long story short<br>So you see<br>So<br>In the end<br>To sum up<br>Summing up<br>To put it in a nutshell<br>In brief | So in short<br>So finally<br>All in all<br>To conclude<br>To summarize<br>To put it into a few words<br>In a nutshell |
| 39) 동의를 나타낼때 | That's right<br>Okay<br>Yes<br>I agree (with you)<br>That's true<br>I guess so | Right<br>Correct<br>Exactly<br>You're right<br>I know |
| | That's just what I was thinking.<br>That's exactly what I was thinking.<br>I couldn't agree with you more.<br>That's exactly what I think.<br>My feelings exactly.<br>You can say that again.<br>I see your point. | <br><br><br>I feel the same way.<br>I'll say<br>That's a good point. |
| 40) 반대를 나타낼때 | That's ridiculous<br>Aw, come on!<br>What! | Are you kidding?<br>What do you mean? |

| | | |
|---|---|---|
| | I don't believe it<br>Are you pulling my leg?<br>I disagree<br>I don't think so | No, definitely not<br>That doesn't fit.<br>I don't agree<br>I don't think that's fair |
| | I'm not sure | I hate to disagree with you, but |
| 41) 불행한 사건에 대해 반응할때 | Oh no<br>What a pity<br>What a nuisance | That's too bad<br>What a shame<br>Poor you |
| | How awful<br>That must have been awful<br>Oh, my God | How terrible<br>I'm sorry to hear that |
| 42) 예상했던(당연한) 불행한 결과에 대한 반응 | It's your own fault<br>That'll teach you<br>What else did you expect? | Someday you'll learn<br>Serves you right |
| 43) 상대방의 말에 흥미를 보일때 | Right<br>Yeah<br>And?<br>Really?<br>And so?<br>Uh-huh | Okay<br>Yes?<br>Well?<br>And then?<br>Mh-hmm |
| 44) 반복을 요청할때 | Pardon me?<br>Could you say that again?<br>Would you repeat that, please?<br>Sorry? | I beg your pardon? |
| | Would you mind repeating that?<br>I didn't catch that last part.<br>Sorry, I don't follow you.<br>I didn't get that. | You lost me there<br>What's that again?<br>I'm lost. |
| 45) 전화상에서 상대방에게 반복을 요구할때 | Sorry, what did you say?<br>I'm sorry I didn't understand that.<br>Do you mind repeating that?<br>Can you repeat that for me, please?<br>Sorry? | Pardon? |

| | | |
|---|---|---|
| 46) 상대방의 이해정도를 확인할 때 | Are you following me?<br>Is that clear?<br>Are you coming along fine?<br>Got it? | Are you with me?<br>Okay so far?<br>Do you understand so far?<br>Right? |
| 47) 상대방의 칭찬에 대한 답을 할때 | Oh, thank you<br>Kind of you to say that<br>Do you really think so?<br>I'm flattered.<br>That's nice to hear | Oh, thanks<br>That's very kind of you<br>Thanks, I needed that.<br>Oh, I'm glad you think so. |
| 48) 더이상 이야기할 시간이 없을때 | Sorry, I've got to go<br>I must be going<br>I hope you don't mind, but | I have to run<br>Would you excuse me, please? |
| 49) 전화한 사람이 끊을려고 할때 | I'd better let you go<br>I know you are busy, so I'll let you go<br>It's been good talking to you | Thanks for your time |
| 50) 전화 받은 사람이 끊을려고 할때 | Well, thanks for calling<br>I'm afraid I don't have time to talk<br>I appreciate your calling | |

# LIS KOREA에서 나온 DISCUSSION TEXTBOOK

## LIS KOREA는 토론 학습 교재 전문 출판사 입니다.

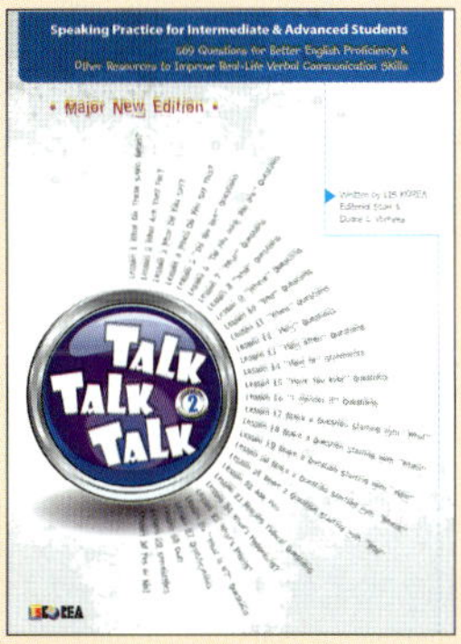


자유토론을 위한 훈련과정

### Talk Talk Talk (1), (2)

- Express Yourself/Let's talk/What Do You Think? 과정을 무리없이 이수하기 위한 예비단계로서 자유토론에 대비하기 위한 많은 훈련과정을 포함하고 있다.
- 여러상황에 맞는 다양한 질문을 학생들에게 던짐으로서 질문과 응답들의 패턴을 이해하고 습득케 하고자 했다.
- Express Yourself/Let's talk/What Do You Think?의 주요 훈련 목표중 하나인 어떤 영어 단어나 문장을 토론자 스스로 다시 설명하는 훈련에 중점을 두었다.

청소년을 위한 토론교재

### New Teen Talk (1), (2)

- 청소년 토론교재의 최고 높은 단계의 교재로서 각권 15개의 이슈속에 500개 이상의 토론주제를 제시합니다.
- 각 권에 포함된 9개의 포멧은 (What Does It Mean? /Comprehension/Teen Talk / Opinion Samples/ Dialog/ Read& Discuss/ Pictures Talk / What's Your Advice? /Synopsis/) 각각의 특징에 맞는 다양하고 흥미로운 토론 주제를 제공합니다.

재미있는 창작 이야기로 토론의 즐거움을

### LET'S TALK FUNNY

- 70개의 재미있는 창작 이야기가 수 백 개의 토론 이슈와 어우러져 독자들에게 재미있게 영어로 토론 할 수 있는 기회를 제공합니다.
- 또한 우리생활에 감추어져 있던 또 다른 50개의 Thinking Points를 제공하여 발상을 전환할 수 있는 계기가 되도록 했습니다.

# Let's Talk (2)

초판 6쇄 인쇄 : 2013년 5월 1일 인쇄
초판 6쇄 발행 : 2013년 5월 5일 발행
지 은 이 : 리스코리아 편집부 & Duane Vorhees
그 림 : 일러스트레이터 박희정
편집디자인 : 예림칼라
펴 낸 곳 : (도서출판) 리스코리아
펴 낸 이 : 조은예
등 록 : 남양주 제 399-2011-000003호
전 화 : (0502) 423-7947
팩 스 : (0502) 423-7948
www.liskorea.co.kr